Go Global

How to take your business
to the world

By Emma Jones

HARRIMAN HOUSE LTD
3A Penns Road
Petersfield
Hampshire
GU32 2EW
GREAT BRITAIN
Tel: +44 (0)1730 233870
Fax: +44 (0)1730 233880
Email: enquiries@harriman-house.com
Website: www.harriman-house.com

Published by Brightword Publishing
Website: www.brightwordpublishing.com

First published in Great Britain in 2010
Copyright © Harriman House Ltd
The right of Emma Jones to be identified as Author has been asserted in accordance
with the Copyright, Design and Patents Act 1988.

ISBN: 978-1908003-00-3

Printed and bound by CPI Antony Rowe.

About the Author

Emma Jones is founder of Enterprise Nation (www.enterprisenation.com), a business expert and author of bestselling books *Spare Room Start Up* and *Working 5 to 9*.

Emma's roots lie in international trade. After studying Law and Japanese at university (and starting her first business during a year's stay in Tokyo) Emma joined international accounting firm Arthur Andersen, and launched an inward investment group to cater for the firm's multinational clients moving to the UK.

Five years later and buoyed by the excitement of the dot-com boom, Emma left the firm to launch Techlocate.com, the UK's first online inward investment advisor. Within two years, Techlocate was successfully sold, and Emma launched Enterprise Nation, a company focused on helping people start and grow a small business.

And so she has come full circle. With a background of helping large businesses invest in the UK, this book is all about helping small businesses export out of the UK.

Certain things have changed – from big business to small business, from inward investment to outbound – but what hasn't changed is Emma's belief that the web makes international trade available to all who seek to take advantage of it.

This book is dedicated to Tony Morris, former Principal of Concord College.

Thank you for accepting me into a place of learning that spawned an interest in international trade and travel. It is to you I owe my wandering feet and mind.

Who This Book is For

Written after months of research and interviews conducted in all corners of the globe, this book is intended for:

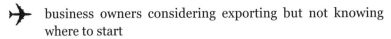 business owners considering exporting but not knowing where to start

business owners already making international sales and wanting to grow further.

You may be a sole trader, a freelancer or a limited company of one and think international trade is beyond your means and resources. Read on and think again!

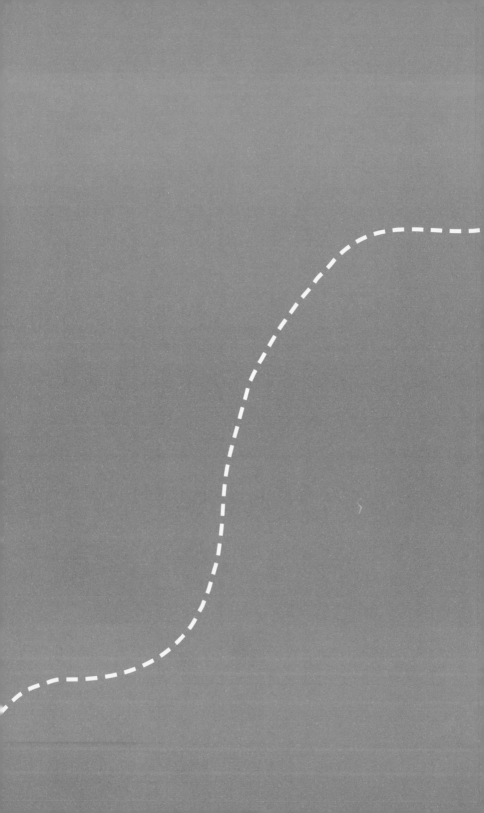

Contents

Introduction   ix
With thanks   xi

Part I: A Whole New World   **1**

✈   Reasons to *Go Global*   3

✈   Crisis of confidence   10

✈   Bring down the barriers   16

Part II: Route Map   **21**
Five steps to success   **23**

Step 1: Research   **23**

✈   Reactive   24

✈   Proactive   24

✈   Government support   30

Step 2: Promote   **34**

✈   Create content and micro publish   34

✈   Distribute and promote   39

✈   Press releases and events   57

Step 3: Sell   **68**

✈   Via your own site   68

✈   Via platform sites   77

✈   Agents and distributors   95

✈   Accepting payment   99

Step 4: Deliver 104

✈ Shipping and postage 104

✈ Administration 115

✈ Distance selling regulations 120

✈ Customer service 123

Step 5: Go Local 128

✈ Website localisation and geo-targeting 128

✈ Local presence 135

✈ Visiting and business etiquette 140

Part III: Where to Go for Help 149

✈ Government support 151

✈ Private sector providers 158

✈ Conclusion 165

Appendices 167

✈ Appendix 1: Country profiles for the UK's top 30 export nations 169

✈ Appendix 2: International trade bodies for the UK's top 30 export nations 223

✈ Appendix 3: Customs declaration forms 227

✈ Appendix 4: World time zones 229

✈ Appendix 5: Cultural briefing 231

Index 233

Other books by Emma Jones 239

Introduction

The decision to write this book was made on Monday 14 September 2009. It was a bright day and the start of a nationwide business road trip; first stop – Glasgow. There I met with Emma Henderson and our conversation went a little like this:

Emma H: "I import fair trade bags from India, apply unique screen print designs, and sell the finished product via my Etsy store to customers in America."

Emma J: "So you're telling me you operate a global business from your spare room in a Glasgow apartment?"

Emma H: "I've never thought of it like that but yes, I guess I do."

Emma's company could rightly be called a mini multinational, and I realised that day what potential there was for thousands more businesses to join her in this; to embrace the web and trade with the world, to leapfrog a potentially slow-growing domestic market and go straight to a global audience, no matter the size of the enterprise.

There were no barriers in sight and Emma was a case in point. Having just graduated from college, she was applying skills in screen printing to build a business. Before that business was even registered she had learnt about export documentation from the UPS delivery man, used her dad's Airmiles to get to trade shows, and made sales to customers in Asia and America. Who would not welcome this exciting new world of trade opportunity, I wondered?

Yet the more I researched the topic, the more I discovered that company owners wanted to expand overseas but were being held back by *perceived* difficulties.

So that's why this book exists. It has been written to dispel the perceptions surrounding international trade. It has been written to tell Emma Henderson's story, along with those of other successful exporters. And it has been written to offer a route map that shows you how to go global, grow your business, and broaden your horizons.

Use it as your guide. It will get you started on the road to international trade and point you in the direction of those who can help along the way.

There's no time like the present to Go Global and take your business to the world.

Emma Jones

emma@enterprisenation.com
twitter.com/emmaljones

With thanks

This book would not have been possible without time and support given by professional experts, successful international traders and private sector providers. My thanks to:

Experts and contributors

Jacqui Allan	British Council
Michael Alliston	Isle of Man, Department of Economic Development
Christine Armistead	UK Trade and Investment
Maggie Choo	Alibaba.com
Raj Dey	Enternships.com
Jody Ford	eBay
Norma Foster	Export Advisor
Nate Gilmore	Shipwire.com
Ian Hendry	WeCanDoBiz
Jessica Houghton	Expert Language Solutions
Grainne Kelly	Bubble Bum
Christine Losecaat	UK China Partners
Doug Mahoney	UK Trade and Investment
Nick McInnes	UK Trade and Investment
Molly Morgan	Alibaba.com
Richard Moross	Moo.com
Ellen Pack	Elance.com
Chris Parker	Harriman House
Doug Richard	School for Startups

San Sharma	Enterprise Nation
Matt Stinchcomb	Etsy.com
Colleen Susini	Regus
Gary Swart	ODesk
Gordon Tempest-Hay	Blue Rubicon
Liz Wald	Etsy.com
Rosa Wilkinson	UK Trade & Investment

Case study companies

Kenneth Benning	Quintessentially Gourmand
Sam Bompas	Bompas and Parr
Simon Burke	Ollie and Forbes
Sarah Cooper	Cows from my Window
Gillian Crawford	Tartan Twist
Rowena Dugdale	Red Ruby Rose
Jane Field	Jonny's Sister
Gerlinde Gniewosz	Zuztertu
Emma Henderson	Showpony
Paul King	Onedaylater.com
Janan Leo	CocoRose London
Marty Mannering	Goeco Electric Transport
Murray Newlands and Luke Brynley-Jones	Influence People
John Pemberton	Give Me Designer Clothing Global
Ruby Pseudo	Ruby Pseudo
Amanda Ruiz	Peruvian Knitwear

Ann-Maree Morrison	Labels4kids.co.uk
Raoul Tawadey	Circalit.com
Lee Torrens	Microstock Diaries
Louise Unger	The Camouflage Company

Private sector supporters

Alibaba.com

HP

PayPal

Powa.com

Regus

Shipwire.com

And finally ...

Thanks to the Enterprise Nation community. Thanks to you for completing the *Go Global* survey, responding to tweets, and posting your comments. The website and this book would not be what it is without you.

Part I:

A Whole New World

Reasons to *Go Global*

This book has been written to help you take your business to the world and there's never been a better time to have this on the agenda. Here's why:

1. Market opportunity

In 2010 the UK faced budget cuts and pay freezes, and business owners were staring at a domestic market that wasn't what it once was. The situation was summed up by Ernst & Young in their ITEM Club Spring 2010 report:

> "2010 will be a gloomy year for consumers, with disposable incomes flat and spending increasing by just 0.5%. With government also retrenching, GDP is forecast to grow by just 1% this year.
>
> Further growth is dependent on the UK increasing its overseas earnings to replace the massive overseas borrowing that financed the 'noughties'. UK Plc needs to develop new markets, especially in fast-growing emerging economies, and to finance overseas expansion and new export capacity in order to provide the economy with an export-led revival from 2011."

So an opportunity for business owners is to open up new markets. The good news is we have the means to access these markets (see 'Technology' section) and they are home to millions of online and consuming customers:

 By the end of the first quarter of 2010, there were 484.97 million broadband subscribers worldwide, up 3.2% on the previous quarter and a figure that continues to increase.

Source: Point Topic

 Global monthly internet traffic in 2010 was two-thirds higher than in 2009.

Source: Cisco

➤ US e-commerce will hit almost $250 billion in 2014, up from $155 billion in 2009.

Source: Internet World Stats

➤ Growth for Western Europe is expected to be even greater, with a predicted increase in the e-commerce market from $93 billion in 2009 to $156 billion in 2014.

Source: Forrester Research

➤ E-commerce will continue to be one of the fastest growing retail channels, with a 2009 European Commission Report showing nearly one-third of individuals in the EU27 member states shopped online and 51% of retailers sold online.

Source: The European Consumer Centre

➤ With over 2 million internet users (equal to a third of the nation's adults online) Egyptians collectively spent $2.1bn online in 2008. The value of e-commerce in China was over US$36bn in 2009, or 1.7% of disposable income; proving there's still plenty of room for growth.

Source: The Digital Economy Rankings and China Internet Network Information Center

An increasing number of people buying online makes for an enormous, worldwide, lucrative market. The potential is significant when you take into account the low base from which we are starting. Research from Eurostat shows that the majority of turnover from e-commerce in the UK (83%) comes from sales within the UK, 11% is from the EU, leaving only 6% from the rest of the world.

This highlights a major opportunity; an opportunity to increase that 6% of non-EU sales and start selling to the world. I pose the question asked by Google on their Export Advisor service:

There are 1.2 billion online consumers around the world. Wouldn't you like to add some of them to your customer base?

If your plan is to increase sales, it's time to look beyond the UK. Selling across borders is the wisest route to take.

> "With the internet making it possible for SMEs to export around the world, overseas sales are big business. In cash terms, exports make up one in six sales for British online businesses."
>
> *– eBay Online Business Index, summer 2009*

2. Exchange rates

Not only are markets outside the UK large and untapped, any weakness in the pound creates a prime time for exporting as your prices become more competitive.

If the pound falls and is weak against other global currencies, it sounds like bad news, but the good news is it makes British products and services cheaper for overseas buyers. The Bank of Scotland claims the weakness of sterling seen in 2010 encouraged its customers to consider trading overseas, and during his time as international trade minister, Lord Davies was quoted as saying:

> "The fall in the pound has provided a window of opportunity for the British exporter, giving them an edge on price. It will enable them to develop initial supply chains and give the foot in the door they need to prove the quality and sophistication of our goods and services."

In May 2010, results from the Purchasing Managers Index, which measures manufacturing and export orders, recorded its highest level of activity since the measurement began in 1996, demonstrating the impact of a weak pound on export activity. The currency situation is a market opportunity that all businesses can take advantage of.

See pages 170 to 222 for a listing of local currencies in the UK's top 30 exporting nations. Good up-to-the-minute currency converters are built into Google, Yahoo and Apple's Mac Dashboard.

3. Diversify and innovate

Small businesses do not want to keep all custom in one geographic area or with one client and international trade allows you to diversify and innovate. A move into new markets is likely to involve learning new ways of doing business, and this is good for company innovation and the bottom line.

66 Exposing a business to overseas competition makes it more competitive, more productive and better equipped to deal with the challenges of globalisation. 99

– Digby Jones, former trade minister

Fast Fact:

The UK sold £4.82bn of food and non-alcoholic drinks overseas in the first six months of 2010.

"British sausages are going down a storm in Germany – with a 410% surge in sales. And the French are snapping up our cheese, boosting cheddar exports by 56% as Europeans cash in on the weak pound. At that rate exports could hit a record £10bn."

Source: Food and Drink Federation featured in *The Mirror*, October 2009, 'British sausage sales are soaring in Germany'

4. Technology

Nothing has enabled international trade more than technology. Having an online presence means reaching a global audience, and technological tools and applications offer cost-effective ways to secure customers and communicate easily with them.

Research shows that almost three-quarters of exporters now use the internet to target customers, with the next choice being through agents and brokers (14%) or using a distribution firm overseas (14%).

eBay is an international mega mall that has helped many businesses go global (see the story of John Pemberton on page 82). The site claims that sales from UK traders to the US have increased by more than a third, and that sales to Australia are up by over a quarter. Despite the recession, says eBay, exports by UK online businesses rose by over 10% between 2008 and 2009, which is almost double the rate of growth of UK sales.

Alibaba is another site that has opened up international trade opportunities. Director Maggie Choo comments:

"Alibaba.com has made the process simple and efficient for anyone to try their hand at international trading. It costs nothing to set up an account and get started. Many users find this is the first step on a journey that delivers significant extra revenue. We already have some 700,000 UK companies trading across the platform and we look forward to helping many more tap into the world's trading opportunities."

Time zones are irrelevant when using online customer service tools and keeping in touch is a breeze with free conference calling and project management software. The technology is now at our fingertips, making sales and communication possible whether you're in Bangor or Bangalore, York or New York.

See pages 77 to 95 for descriptions of other international sales platforms and all sections for technology tools and tips.

"The internet is now fundamental to commercial success and social prosperity."

– *Digital Economy Rankings 2010*

"Increasingly, small businesses do not start off trading locally as they did in the past. If you have a website you can think globally from the beginning."

– *Clive Lewis, head of enterprise, Institute of Chartered Accountants for England and Wales*

5. Political will

Political leaders across the globe are setting goals on exports and international trade.

In March 2010, in his state of the union address, US President Barack Obama unveiled the National Export Initiative and announced a target to double exports from the US by 2015:

"The National Export Initiative will help meet my administration's goal of doubling exports over the next five years by working to remove trade barriers abroad, by helping firms – especially small businesses – overcome the hurdles to entering new export markets, by assisting with financing, and in general by pursuing a government-wide approach to export advocacy abroad."

In Europe, Viviane Reding, EU commissioner for information society and media, has called for a digital single market as a top priority, saying:

"We won't have a real digital economy until we remove all barriers to online transactions, also for end-consumers. This must be on top of the list of all policy initiatives to relaunch the single market project."

And back in the UK, the prime minister and foreign secretary stand firmly behind export as a policy to improve the country's economic wellbeing and social standing. This is reflected in David Cameron's early trade visits to the US, Turkey and India, as well as comments from William Hague on Britain's place in a networked world.

❝ As a new government, we are absolutely focused on reopening Britain for business. We want to make Britain the best possible place to invest in and to trade with. **❞**

– David Cameron, during a visit to the US, July 2010

Fine words from politicians and we welcome seeing them put into practice!

6. Broadened horizons

Doing business overseas is not necessarily all about business. Through trade connections you meet people with whom you may not ordinarily have come across and travel to places you may not have thought to visit.

❝ Ensure you choose a territory that is right for your offer but, importantly, one that you like. Hopefully, you will be spending a lot of time there. **❞**

– Christine Losecaat, managing director of Little Dipper and chair of UK China Partners

In the process of growing your business, there is a chance to learn new languages, discover lost cultures and eat surprising delicacies. Consider business as the magic carpet that will carry you to adventures in far-off countries, steeped in commercial and cultural opportunity.

Crisis of confidence

The reasons laid out for going global are good ones, and yet despite growing markets, ease of access, political will and the opportunity to broaden horizons, out of a base of 4.5 million-plus small businesses in the UK, **only 75,000** are currently exporting. I believe the figure is low on account of a *crisis of confidence*.

This is reflected in many surveys that show a high number of business owners who *want* to export but are deterred by perceived business barriers.

The HSBC 'Going International' report claims millions of small businesses are unduly sceptical about the importance of international trade. Four-in-ten businesses contemplating international trade see it as potentially crucial to their overall survival, but this number rises to nearly nine-in-ten for those with experience of already trading overseas. Companies that have the confidence to sell abroad are reaping the rewards, with four-in-five saying they consider it to be a profitable venture. 78% of these businesses having grown as a direct consequence.

There's also what Noel Quin, HSBC's UK head of commercial banking, calls a "psychological barrier":

> "The reality of setting up overseas trading deals was perceived as more costly and problematic by potential exporters than was actually the experience of those that already exported. The benefits [of exporting] far outweigh the costs when you start to do it."

Another high street bank, Lloyds TSB Commercial, commissioned similar research and came out with similar results. 'British Businesses Missing a Trick in Export Markets' ran the headline, with the facts as follows:

➤ 62% of SME [small to medium-sized enterprise] exporters have experienced growth in foreign markets in the last 12 months.

➤ 39% of businesses not currently exporting say fearing a lack of demand is the main reason for not doing so.

21% cite worries about late payments as a reason for not exporting.

"By far the biggest concern amongst small businesses questioned was that there would not be demand for their product or service overseas. And yet, amongst firms that are exporting, overseas trade is contributing to a growing proportion of company turnover with almost nine out of ten believing exports as a percentage of turnover will increase this year, or at least stay at current levels."

This crisis of confidence has been sufficiently serious for trade Ministers and representatives to step up to the stage and voice concern.

66 UK companies overestimate the barriers and underestimate the benefits of exporting. I've been disappointed by the fact that although we are a nation of small and medium-sized businesses, we are not yet a nation of exporters. 99

– Lord Davies, former minister of international trade

66 Business needs to rediscover the mercantile spirit that has driven our wealth in the past and now drives other, younger industrial economies. 99

– David Frost, director general, British Chambers of Commerce

66 Future economic prosperity will only come from UK companies exploiting opportunities overseas. 99

– Andrew Cahn, chief executive, UK Trade and Investment

66 The only way the UK will recover quickly and sustainably from the recession is by trading her way out. That calls for our continued, indeed our increased, commitment to the export of goods and services. 99

– Digby Jones, former international trade minister

There is a common thread to these protestations. It is a call to action for companies to overcome fear and take our products and services to the world.

But before we look at how to do that, let's examine what's holding us back.

Based on the evidence, I have come up with a list of key deterrents or perceived barriers and divided them into two key categories:

1. Perceptual & psychological
2. Profitable & practical

1. Perceptual & psychological

The UK has a stellar record when it comes to trade, being the world's second largest exporter of commercial services* and the eighth largest exporter of merchandise**. It has one of the highest shares of services as an exporter across the globe. But my question to you is this: when you think of the word 'export' or the concept of 'going global', what comes to mind?

I will hazard a guess it is:

 big business and large investment

 cargo and freight

manufacturing and machinery

capital and infrastructure.

International trade carries with it the perception of being a heavy-duty task taken on by big companies with deep pockets. This is even reflected in the way we measure exports and the imagery that goes with it.

The international trade page on the Business Link website (www.businesslink.gov.uk) shows a large ship carrying big boxes, ploughing its way through choppy seas. The key export indicator as measured by the Office for National Statistics is 'The Monthly Review of External Trade Statistics' which notes oil, manufacturing, chemicals, road vehicles and power-generating equipment as top exports from the UK. There is little reference to the volume of smaller items sold via the web and packages shipped via the local Post Office.

Despite the fact this perception no longer matches reality, small business owners are put off, with exporting made to look an intensive and expensive affair.

* World Trade Organisation
** OECD Factbook 2008

"While exporting may have traditionally been seen as only suitable to companies in industries such as manufacturing, firms operating in other sectors have the opportunity to explore new markets and assess international demand for their products."

– Donald Kerr, commercial banking director, Bank of Scotland

Many business owners speak of 'fear of the unknown' when it comes to doing business with people they don't know in countries they've never visited and in languages of which they have little knowledge.

Certainly, international trade forces us out of our comfort zone. But what it does do is introduce us to new territories and ideally, lucrative ones!

"Despite an insatiable consumer appetite in China and India, companies dipping their toes into international waters are opting to trade much closer to home. **"**

– HSBC 'Going International' report

2. Profitable & practical

You want to know that time invested is time well spent. Small businesses have doubts over:

➤ how to cost-effectively find and communicate with customers abroad

➤ how to guarantee payment amidst currency fluctuations

➤ what the general cost of exporting is, when taking into account shipping and international travel.

"Trepidation is founded on issues like geographical distance, language and cultural differences and occasionally market access barriers. It's about having the confidence to visualise yourself doing business outside the UK."

– Lord Davies, former trade minister

When it comes to matters of a practical nature, this category is an umbrella for a number of fears, including how to go about identifying overseas customers, tackling legislation and paperwork, language and cultural barriers, and where to go for help.

> **66** 41% of small businesses not trading internationally view the language barrier as the key inhibitor in taking their businesses overseas. **99**
>
> – HSBC 'Going International' report

There's even the practicality of air travel, with the 2010 volcanic ash cloud having had such an impact that 16% of companies said they would reconsider overseas trade on account of the disruption it can be subject to.

In December 2009, trading platform Alibaba.com questioned 3,600 entrepreneurs about sources of help and advice. The results revealed that 98% of respondents were unaware of initiatives to facilitate international trade.

Evidence given to the National Audit Office by CBI emphasised the same issue:

> "A cry we often hear, particularly from small and medium-sized companies is that, 'I just didn't know that this was a service which was available to me'."

And in our own 'Going Global' survey carried out on Enterprise Nation, 79% of respondents said they did not know that public support for international trade promotion was available.

This has been acknowledged by national government body UK Trade & Investment (UKTI), which, with an annual budget at its disposal of £268 million, is charged with attracting inward investment to the UK and boosting exports from the UK.

Indeed, the agency's own research:

> "indicates large numbers of existing exporters are not aware UKTI exists or are not convinced of the potential benefits from any external assistance, suggesting that many businesses have yet to access the services provided by UK Trade & Investment."

Actions are being taken to raise its profile, but UKTI will want to be sure their programmes are well-suited to the needs of modern day global traders who tend not to have employees, export departments or years of trading history, all of which currently form the eligibility criteria of key programmes such as Passport to Export.

On page 18 I offer thoughts on how government support could be better structured to suit the modern-day trading business, and pages 151 to 157 provide outlines of programmes on offer from UKTI and devolved bodies in Scotland, Wales and Northern Ireland, as well as other organisations that can help.

As a beginner's guide, this book has been written to get you started on the right foot and with all the resources you need to prosper as you start to export to the world. If you have felt any of the fears raised above, don't worry, as we will be busting the myths they depend on, and bringing down the barriers that may be holding you back from profitably taking your own business global.

“ I see fear stopping people making sales. To them I'd like to say don't let fear of the unknown or prejudice hold back your business – widen your market, spread your wings! **”**

– Mhairi Gordon, Impact Associates

Bring down the barriers!

It's time to face the fear and fight back with reality; the reality of international trade according to the businesses profiled in this book and people who responded to our *Go Global* survey held in July 2010.

Fears and realities

Fear: To trade successfully overseas, I first have to trade in my own market for years.

Reality: 28% of the companies surveyed and profiled started selling overseas within 12 months of trading and for 36% it was between one and two years. The companies were discovered via search engines or recommendation, promoted via local blogs and sites, and orders have grown ever since via word of mouth. For the majority of businesses (64%), this happened before their venture turned two years old.

Fear: It will cost me a lot of money to become a global business.

Reality: None of the companies profiled spent a penny, dime or yen on purposefully attracting their first overseas order. With business coming in from overseas customers, they are now investing in having sites translated or making customer visits, but even this can be done on a budget. These companies are all making the most of free or low-cost technology tools and social media to increase orders and customer satisfaction.

Fear: I can't make sales or service customers if I don't have an office overseas.

Reality: Of the businesses surveyed, 62% sell overseas via their own website and 25% sell via other commercial sites such as eBay, Alibaba and Etsy. When you have a presence on the web, you rarely need a physical presence in the country.

Fear: I will need to employ lots of people to help take my business to the world.

Reality: Of the 20 businesses profiled, 35% of them have one employee (the owner) and only 10% have more than 10 employees.

Rather than employing staff, they are outsourcing and subcontracting the work, everything from manufacturing to identifying agents, and finding talent on sites such as Elance, oDesk and LinkedIn.com, from which they can effectively form international project teams. The way to grow, say our profiled businesses, is to focus on the bit you do best and outsource the rest.

Fear: I won't be able to understand export documentation.
Reality: A significant 85% of survey respondents send their products overseas via the local Post Office and 11% use international courier companies, with the remainder making the most of local shipping arrangements. It is from these experts that you will learn all you need to know about documentation and customs procedures.

Fear: I will have to speak the language of the countries to which I'm selling.
Reality: It's a nice touch to learn a few phrases and have parts of your site translated, but until you reach that point, take advice from our profiled success stories, and let Google Translate become your new best friend!

Fear: I won't get paid.
Reality: Of the businesses surveyed, 65% use an online payment gateway such as PayPal to ensure payment is as easy and secure as possible for the customer, regardless of their country or currency. Having these systems in place increases efficiency and reduces the risk of customers holding back on payment.

Fear: I won't convert one international sale into lots more sales.
Reality: Many of the profiled businesses speak of 'accidentally' getting into global trade by virtue of receiving international orders via their website or network. The experience of delivering that first order brings with it confidence in your abilities to service new markets and an appetite for more orders. This explains why 78% of survey respondents believe their international sales will increase over the next 12 months.

Fear: I just don't know where to start.
Reality: Start right here!

How government can help

In researching *Go Global*, I have spoken to many businesses and delved deep into the topic. Based on this I believe there are a number of actions government can take to bring down the barriers to international trade and increase support for small business. Some are macro, others more micro. In brief, they are:

1. Review the criteria for key trade programmes such as Passport to Export and the Export Marketing Research Scheme. Current criteria state that companies must have been trading for more than three years and have over five employees. This would make all the companies profiled in this book ineligible, yet if they received support they may be better placed to boost international orders.

2. Explore new export indicators; a way to count and measure export volumes that better reflects the contribution being made by small businesses selling services and goods via their own and other commercial sites. In China, Alibaba.com provides quarterly reports to the Chinese Government; could the Office for National Statistics source similar stats from the likes of eBay, Alibaba and Etsy? These sites represent powerful barometers of international trade activity.

3. Announcements stating an increased role for the Foreign & Commonwealth Office in trade promotion are welcome. With officers in post often for many years, these well-connected agents on the ground will undoubtedly be an invaluable resource for the small business entering a new and unknown market. Taking this on a stage,

could the FCO develop a *Go Global* app connecting small businesses to local embassies, as well as providing a local news feed/travel information/political updates, etc?

4. Work closer with private sector providers such as the partners on this project who provide valuable services and support to exporting businesses. Both government and corporates have the same objective in mind; encouraging more small businesses to grow through increased international sales. There is indeed scope for joint work.

5. Promote initiatives like this book! Small businesses need encouragement and assistance to take the first step in exporting.

I accept government budgets are not what they once were. These recommendations are made with this in mind. None of them require significant outlay or expense but they will deliver a return on investment in more companies exporting and making the 1.2 billion unreached customers part of their core market.

The single and simple aim of this book is to encourage and assist anyone who is starting and growing a small business to consider overseas sales. Government is in a strong position to do the same.

Part II:

Route Map

Five steps to success

This section shows how you can take your business to the world in five easy steps.

Step 1: Research

Before embarking on any journey, you need to know where you're going and what to do when you get there. Planning for overseas business is just the same. It's important to ask a number of questions to determine if there's a market of people willing and able to buy your goods. The key areas to research are the four Cs:

Countries	Customers
Where is there most likely to be a demand for my product/service? What is the state of the economy and what are the general rules of business? Are there contacts who could offer help/support?	What does my customer profile look like and how many potential customers are there in this market? How do customers in this country like to buy and be served? Which sites do they visit, what kind of media do they consume and who are their key influencers?
Cost	**Competition**
What should I charge for my goods and services in this market bearing in mind existing demand and supply? What are the costs of getting my product/service to this market and delivering follow-up customer support? Taking into account my costs and the level at which I can charge, will I be making a profit?	Who else is servicing the customers I have identified? How do I stand out from the competition, i.e. what is my USP and why will customers buy from me, compared with existing suppliers? Is there potential for a tie-up with others offering similar services and products?

To get to your answers you need to undertake reactive and proactive research:

Reactive

Are you already receiving a number of visitors to your site or orders from certain countries? You can check the origin of site traffic using your site's analytics tool or use Google Analytics (www.google.com/analytics), which is free. If you're seeing high levels of traffic from a country that's not your own, this spells i-n-t-e-r-n-a-t-i-o-n-a-l trade potential.

React in a positive way to existing customers who ask for orders to be shipped overseas or for you to service their contacts, friends and family in other parts of the world. Can you deliver? The answer should be: yes, you can!

> "Research your market, study your customer and know what you are selling is a good product. It was my foreign customers living in the UK that opened the doors for me and encouraged me to look overseas."
>
> – Flore Nzoghe, Bootcharms Designs, www.flore-star.com

Proactive

Source primary and secondary data by carrying out research, either in-house or by outsourcing to a market research company, freelancer in the host country, virtual PA, student or intern. Here's where to go for local knowledge:

Research links for countries and customers

✈ UK Trade & Investment country reports:
www.ukti.gov.uk/export/countries.html

✈ Alibaba country profiles:
news.alibaba.com/country-profiles.html

✈ Alibaba industry reports:
resources.alibaba.com/industry-report.html

✈ British chambers of commerce country reports:
www.link2portal.com/globaltrade

✈ HSBC country guides:
www.business.hsbc.co.uk/1/2/international-business/country-guides

✈ Google's Export Adviser:
www.google.co.uk/exportadviser

✈ UKTI report dedicated to emerging markets:
www.newwavemarkets.com

Fast Fact:

Mexico has free trade agreements with more countries than any other in the world.

Fast Fact:

Google.fr is the most visited website in France, accounting for one in every 10 internet visits. Social networking is more popular in France than in the UK, but online shopping less so.

Source: Hitwise

Turn to page 170 to view country profiles for the top 30 nations exported to from the UK, including links to local news feeds, figures for resident online populations and a few key phrases.

"Although traditional markets in Europe and the US will remain the main targets for most firms, there is real potential across the Middle East and Asia which is as yet untapped."

– Donald Kerr, commercial banking director, Bank of Scotland

Digital nations

If the plan is to sell your product or service online, you need to be selling to a country or countries that boast high levels of online spending and an ease with digital dealings. The digital economy rankings by *The Economist*'s Intelligence Unit assess the quality of a country's ICT infrastructure and allocate scores based on the levels at which consumers and businesses use digital services. In 2010 the top 20 countries in the ranking were:

1.	Sweden
2.	Denmark
3.	United States
4.	Finland
5.	Netherlands
6.	Norway
7.	Hong Kong
8.	Singapore
9.	Australia
10.	New Zealand
11.	Canada
12.	Taiwan
13.	South Korea
14.	United Kingdom
15.	Austria
16.	Japan
17.	Ireland
18.	Germany
19.	Switzerland
20.	France

Source: The digital economy rankings 2010, 'Beyond e-readiness' (**bit.ly/bV13WW**).

Research links for costs

Use the Google Profit Calculator to work out the bottom line and gain confidence that exporting will be a profitable venture: www.google.co.uk/intl/en/exportadviser/the-bottom-line

Weigh up the costs of international postage with this online tool from Royal Mail: bit.ly/NoYub

Check out the costs of travelling, as and when required: www.xe.com/tec/table.shtml

Research links for competition

Visit forums and sites where your potential customers gather, and read up on the local competition. Locate these forums through Google searches and following links posted on social media sites such as Facebook and Twitter.

Fast Fact:

According to eBay, in 2009 the highest number of exports by UK eBay sellers were to the United States (13.7%) and Germany (9.3%).

Trade bodies and international groups can also play an important role in assisting you. Organisations such as JETRO representing Japan, the French Chamber of Commerce and the China-Britain Business Council are on hand and have a deep knowledge of market conditions and customer potential.

See pages 223 to 226 for the trade bodies relevant to the UK's top 30 export countries.

Fast Fact:

The most popular markets for small business owners in the UK considering international trade are France, Germany, Spain and Ireland.

Source: HSBC 'Going International' report

Primary data

Source primary or firsthand data by conducting a survey or posing questions via social media channels.

Survey tools

➤ Surveymonkey (www.surveymonkey.com)

➤ Wufoo (www.wufoo.com)

Social media channels

➤ Twitter (www.twitter.com)

➤ Facebook (www.facebook.com)

➤ LinkedIn (www.linkedin.com)

See pages 43 to 53 for information on how these tools can also promote your business in new markets.

Fast Fact:

India has a population of 1.2 billion and an economy expected to grow at 8% a year for the next 25 years. It is estimated the middle class will be larger than the entire population of the United States by 2015.

Source: *Sunday Times* and UK Trade & Investment

SUCCESS STORY

Gillian Crawford, Tartan Twist

Necklaces, bracelets, earrings and brooches; all made with a stylish and loving touch by a home-based workforce in Scotland. Popular amongst Scottish expats around the world? You bet. And it's a market that Tartan Twist co-founders Gillian Crawford and Lindsay Bowditch are leveraging to their advantage.

The company was receiving a few orders from overseas but it was publicity in *Scottish Field* and the *Sunday Post* (both popular publications with the expat community) that really started to propel sales and opportunities.

> "We were selling our products to the likes of the Scottish Parliament shop, the National Trust for Scotland, the Royal Yacht Britannia, Glasgow Museums and the National Museum of Scotland and realised that with all bases covered in Scotland, we had to look elsewhere for new business."

At a Scottish trade fair, Gillian and Lindsay were approached by a Japanese company that had 20 department store outlets; suddenly they had a serious international customer. The company offered to translate the sales materials into Japanese but what the purchaser was after was something with authentic provenance.

With financial help from Scottish Development International, Gillian was able to travel to the Far East to do the deal and meet other potential buyers.

> "We are fortunate in that we have a defined community, which is Scottish expats and anyone abroad who has a passion for all things made in Scotland. This helps keep our marketing costs low as we promote ourselves through Caledonian Societies and other places where we know Scottish expats gather!"

As well as Japan, Tartan Twist is also selling to individual shops in the US, Canada and Australia. The two founders want to explore potential in the German market where they have seen early signs of interest for their products.

Their site accepts PayPal and credit card payments and recognises the country of origin of the customer, thereby automating whether to charge VAT.

www.tartantwist.com

@tartan_twist

See page 153 for information on how Scottish Development International (www.sdi.co.uk) helps small businesses trade overseas.

Top Tip:

The more you can define your international audience, the lower your marketing costs. Know your new audience well and refine your approach.

Fast Fact:

Over 9 million people in the US claim some kind of Scottish link or ancestry.

Source: Scottish Development International

Government support

The government has two main programmes that support research into potential markets and routes to market. The schemes are:

1. Overseas Market Introduction Scheme (OMIS)

This scheme is intended to ensure that businesses in the UK benefit from the country's extensive network of embassies and commercial offices across the world, harnessing the power of local representatives to carry out research and make local introductions on your behalf. To find out if you are eligible for assistance, contact a local trade advisor in your region.

 Information on OMIS:
www.ukti.gov.uk/export/accessinginternationalmarkets/
overseasmarketintroductionservice.html

 Regional trade advisor contacts:
www.ukti.gov.uk/export/unitedkingdom/contactus.html

2. The Export Marketing Research Scheme (EMRS)

Managed on behalf of UK Trade & Investment by the British Chambers of Commerce, this programme will assist in collating research or will cover part of the cost of paying for a third party to carry out research on your behalf. To be eligible your company should have been trading for more than two years and have more than five employees. See page 152 for more details.

 www.britishchambers.org.uk/zones/export/export-
marketing-research-scheme

See pages 151 to 157 for details of support from government bodies in England, Scotland, Wales and Northern Ireland.

66 I invented my product, which is an inflatable car booster seat for kids, in March 2009 and then flew to China to make the prototype. I applied for my patent and safety tests at the same time and in December2009 began making sales via the website. It was through the site that we had our first contact from the US (the Texas police department got in touch to place an order) and I could see from Google Analytics that we had a lot of traffic from the US. Fast forward to today and I have now moved to America to launch my product directly into this market along with Brazil, Japan and the rest of Europe! **99**

– Grainne Kelly, founder, Bubble Bum

Whether you decide to take this first research step yourself or allocate the job to others, the essential data you're looking for is evidence that you have a product that's priced right and fit for purpose for a market of customers prepared to buy from you rather than the competition. If the research points to a positive result, it's time to start promoting your presence.

Countries courting you!

When researching prospective countries, take into account the level of interest that country has in strengthening trade relationships with you.

Australialive is a month-long celebration of Australian business, culture, food and wine held in the UK, including a forum focused on business opportunities in Australia. Chairman of the project, Phillip Aiken, says:

> "Our goal is to strengthen further our trading ties with the UK and encourage businesses and consumers to discover more about Australia."

The website outlines opportunities available for British businesses, displaying "the scope of what Australia offers as a thriving economy, exciting trading partner and the best holiday destination in the world."

When a country is this keen to do business with the UK, it bodes well for a profitable partnership.

www.australialive.org

Fast Fact:

Singapore is ranked as the world's top country for ease of doing business.

Source: World Bank

SUCCESS STORY

Sam Bompas, Bompas and Parr

Bompas and Parr is the company name for entrepreneurial duo Sam Bompas and Harry Parr, who gave up jobs as a property developer and architect, respectively, to pursue their true love – jelly! Good job they did, as the world would be a blander place without this bright and global business.

Since the launch of Bompas and Parr, the company has rapidly gained a reputation for crafting amazing jelly creations. The founders have expanded into producing bespoke jelly moulds and kitchenalia, as well as providing food and design consultancy to a stellar client list. Since 2009, Bompas and Parr have turned their attention overseas.

"In 2009, we focused on the US market, [in 2010] we've made waves in Europe and the plan for 2011 is to raise our profile in Asia. We do this through going to cookery shows, being seen in the media, and lecturing about jelly. This activity has resulted in us working for the likes of Kraft, a restaurant in Singapore and the San Francisco Museum of Modern Art."

The relationship with Kraft is a close one, involving weekly conversations with the head of development at what is the world's largest jelly retailer. For their next trick, Bompas and Parr are working with international neuroscientists to concoct a jelly that responds to your brain waves.

"If I'm honest, we still marvel at the fact we've managed to build a business out of something we enjoy so much. But the secret to our success is in the niche we have created. If you want a jelly experience, making it or admiring it, we have become the go-to company and as we're currently the only one in the world, it means we happen to attract quite a bit of international attention."

www.jellymongers.co.uk

Step 2: Promote

Having identified your new markets and countries, the next step is to get noticed. And the easiest way to raise profile on a worldwide scale is to have a precise understanding of your product or service and the audience to whom you wish to appeal. In other words, the best way to promote yourself (and keep costs as low as possible) is to **focus on your niche and build global reach**.

I will show you how to achieve this in two moves that are both time and cost-effective. They apply whether you are selling a product or a service. Here's what to do:

1   create content and micro-publish

2. distribute and promote.

Create content and micro publish

I'm talking about content that defines your brand and tells your story. Customers like to receive content in a number of sensory ways; they like to be informed and entertained, they like to see, read, listen and watch. Affordable technology means you can now appeal to all their senses, no matter where customers are located. Achieve this by becoming a 'micro-publisher' – this involves developing content around your product or service and then publishing, distributing and promoting this content via your own site and through social media networks.

10 routes to publishing

1. Write a blog – become the known expert in your field by writing a blog dedicated to the topic. See page 89 to read how Lee Torrens has become a world expert in micro stock photography and how his blog led to opportunities he never imagined. To start quickly and easily, visit Blogger or Wordpress and get posting!

✈ Blogger (www.blogger.com)

✈ Wordpress (www.wordpress.com)

✈ Wordpress Global Translator – Wordpress plugin that translates your blog into 48 languages (wordpress.org/extend/plugins/global-translator)

2. *Publish a book* – become a published author on the topic of your choice by self-publishing via sites such as Lulu, Blurb and Snapfish by HP. Utilise the book as a business development tool, printing on demand to take copies to events, and offering free and downloadable versions to potential customers. Being an author gives you credibility and gives customers information and insight. It's also worth contacting publishers directly. They're often happy to talk to authors – and don't all insist on an agent!

✈ Blurb (www.blurb.com)

✈ Lulu.com (www.lulu.com)

✈ Snapfish by HP (www.snapfish.co.uk)

✈ Brightword Publishing (www.brightwordpublishing.com)

Brightword is the company that published this book. It's a company focused on producing books, kits and digital products for anyone starting and growing a small business. If you have a proposal, please get in touch!

3. *Present yourself* – put yourself forward to speak at events overseas (consider asking for a fee and/or costs to be covered – see page 143 for a travel cost calculator) or suggest being a satellite speaker where you are beamed into the conference hall via video link-up, so saving the effort and expense of travel. Invite customers and prospects and make the presentation openly available via Slideshare.

✈ Slideshare.com (www.slideshare.com)

4. *Host a webinar* – share your expertise or demonstrate a process by hosting a webinar or visual presentation where a 'live' audience can see you and interact. Achieve this via platforms such as GoToWebinar, Webex and DimDim, and remember to host it at a time that suits your target audience, allowing for time differences and availability.

➤ GoToMeeting (www.gotomeeeting.com) and GoToWebinar (www.gotomeeting.com/fec/webinar)

➤ Webex (www.webex.co.uk)

➤ DimDim (www.dimdim.com)

➤ Yugma (www.yugma.com)

See page 125 for information on how collaborative websites can help international teams work across borders.

5. *Produce a film* – maybe the word 'film' is a little ambitious but you can create your own video content with a Flip camera or by hiring in a cameraman and having a sponsored series of guides that can be uploaded to video sharing sites such as YouTube, Vimeo and eHow.

➤ Flip camera (www.theflip.com)

➤ YouTube (www.youtube.com)

➤ Vimeo (www.vimeo.com)

➤ eHow (www.ehow.co.uk)

See page 53 for an overview of using YouTube as a promotional platform.

7. *Broadcast a podcast* – for customers who like to listen to what you have to say at a time that suits them, upload a podcast with top tips, interviews and your thoughts of the day. Make it available on your site, iTunes and Podcast Alley to be sure of a wide audience. Follow advice from podcast producer San Sharma on how to record a podcast on a Skype call (see page 38).

➤ Submit a podcast to the iTunes store (www.apple.com/itunes/podcasts/specs.html)

➤ Podcast Alley (www.podcastalley.com)

8. *Deliver training* – whether your skill is in embroidering handmade shoes or developing stylish websites, your knowledge could be shared with others. Rather than seeing this as surrendering intelligence to potential competitors, offer instruction you're comfortable with that will create fans and followers who will learn

from you, buy from you and, critically, encourage others to do the same. Check out platforms GoToTraining and Webtraining, encourage contacts to sign up and then after the demonstration you have a chance to follow up with a group of new contacts.

✈ GoToTraining
(www.gotomeeting.com/fec/training/online_training)

✈ WebEx Webtraining
(www.webex.co.uk/product-overview/training-center)

66 Companies attending my School for Startups events come with a global mindset and with the intention to serve global markets. The lessons I teach are how to promote yourself to that market and service it well. My own business is expanding overseas; into South America, Romania and beyond. The more I come into contact with small business owners the more I see how bright the prospects are for increasing trade across borders. 99

– Doug Richard, founder, School for Startups www.schoolforstartups.com

9. *Form groups* – encourage others to discuss, debate and contribute to your content by forming groups utilising social media platforms such as Facebook, LinkedIn and Ning. Bonding interested people to each other will bond them ever closer to you; the content creator and group host.

✈ Facebook (www.facebook.com)

✈ LinkedIn (www.linkedin.com)

✈ Ning (www.ning.com)

See pages 43 to 52 for details on how Facebook and LinkedIn can be used to promote your business.

10. *Develop an app*

Take your content and make an iPhone app with browser-based platform Appmakr.

66 AppMakr can be used by anyone with existing content and fans or customers to reach; bloggers/writers, business owners, website owners.... 99

– AppMakr.com

It's free to use and you can either set a list price to make sales via the App Store or make it available free of charge.

 Appmakr (www.appmakr.com)

How to record a podcast on a Skype call

You can produce a podcast interview using Skype, Pamela Call Recorder, and a little editing know-how. San Sharma shows how it's done in five simple steps

1. Sign up for a free Skype account at (www.skype.com) and download the Skype software.

2. If you're using a Windows machine, download Pamela Call Recorder (www.pamela.biz) which lets you record your Skype calls. If you're on a Mac, you can download Call Recorder for Skype (www.ecamm.com). Both have free trial versions, but only cost around £13 when that's expired.

3. Call up your interviewee using Skype. If they're a Skype user too, that will be a free call but if they're on a fixed or mobile line, you'll need to get some Skype Credit (www.skype.com/intl/en/prices/skype-credit).

4. Once you've made a connection and agreed with the interviewee the format of the conversation, hit the record button on your call recorder software and you're off!

5. Edit using Audacity (audacity.sourceforge.net), which is free for Windows and Macs, or with GarageBand (www.apple.com/ilife/garageband), which comes with most Macs (you can also buy it as part of the iLife package). And the easiest way to share your recording is by uploading it to AudioBoo (www.audioboo.com), which lets people listen to it on the web, embedded on your website or via iTunes or a mobile phone.

San Sharma is community manager at Enterprise Nation (www.enterprisenation.com)

Price point

You have two pricing options when offering content via these ten publishing channels:

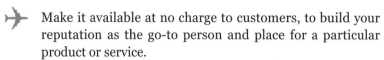 Make it available at no charge to customers, to build your reputation as the go-to person and place for a particular product or service.

Charge for access/downloads/viewing and turn your micro-publishing activity into a revenue stream in its own right.

Individual judgement will be needed in this and it's something you can assess over time. Start with a mix of charged-for and free content, ensure you are providing good value and incentives for your community to remain engaged, and the options to introduce charged-for content will increase.

Distribute and promote

With your content formed and packaged, you want people from across the world to visit, consume, and participate. Attract an audience through promotion both online and off.

International search engine optimisation

This is setting up your website so that online consumers discover it when they type items and keywords into search engines – you want to be the business found if the descriptive keyword(s) describe your speciality. This can be achieved through international search engine optimisation, commonly known as international SEO, and your content provides an important role here.

❝ International search engine optimisation (SEO) is all about getting your website found by potential customers in your target countries who are searching using their local search engines. Quite simply, if you want to get new business in France, then you want your website to rank well in the French version of Google. ❞

– Susan Hallam, international SEO expert

SEO is an important part of your promotional toolkit as people increasingly go online as their first step in locating products and services. According to comScore, over 113 billion searches were conducted globally during July 2009, up 41% on the year before:

> "Latin America exhibited the most searches per person with an average of 130 searches per searcher. Europe had the second highest overall search volume per person with 117 searches per searcher, followed by North America with 112."

Investigate the search engines that are most popular in the territory to which you'd like to sell. Google continues to dominate the global search market, accounting for 67% of all queries worldwide, but there are other engines to bear in mind. For example, Baidu (www.baidu.com) wins the title of most popular search engine in China, with 55% market share, and the same goes for Yandex (www.yandex.com/ru) in Russia.

Register your site with the major search engines to increase the chances of it appearing in results.

 Google (www.google.com/addurl)

 Bing (www.bing.com/webmaster)

 Yahoo (siteexplorer.search.yahoo.com)

 Baidu (for China) (www.baidu.com/search/url_submit – requires Chinese translator)

 The Open Directory Project (www.dmoz.org/add.html)

See pages 170 to 222 for country profiles of the UK's top 30 export locations with details of local search engines.

Optimise your site by having keywords you think overseas customers will be searching for. It also helps to have your site registered with a country-specific top level domain. See pages 128 to 132 for details on country specific domains and how to localise your website. Stay up-to-date with the most popular terms being searched for on the web by visiting www.searchenginewatch.com and clicking on 'Ratings and Stats'.

For more detailed information on international SEO, Susan Hallam's whitepaper is a good place to start (www.shcl.co.uk/wp-content/uploads/2010/07/International-SEO1.pdf) and check out these sources of industry research:

 Search Laboratory (www.searchlaboratory.com)

 Global Strategies International (www.globalstrategies.com)

Susan Hallam (www.shcl.co.uk)

Google juice

If you run Google AdWords campaigns on the UK site, consider extending them to take into account Google searches in your new market(s). Use Google Translate (**translate.google.com**) but also check with linguists or locals to ensure the translation is culturally correct as well as technically in order. Check to see how the site is performing by using 'Advance Search' from the Google home page and click on 'region' to choose your preferred country. Also visit **prchecker.info** and **pagerankalert.com** to check support for individual web pages.

"With International SEO, all of the site specific and page coding issues are the same as a single language strategy, but content, language, and keyword phrases must be made relevant to the local searcher."

– *Global Strategies International*

Coming up the ranks

Write content, identify influencers and get listed to improve your chances of appearing higher up in local search results:

➤ Write original content for your own site and for others; ideally, post something every couple of days so the search engine spiders pick you up in their trawls around the web.

➤ Identify influential bloggers and sites in your trade/industry that are popular in the countries in which you want to do business, contact them and offer to write posts. You can also improve your visibility by writing helpful comments in forums and on other people's posts.

➤ Secure links to and from popular and quality sites and consider listing your business in directories that have global appeal such as Google Places (**www.google.com/local/add/businesscenter**) and Google Shops (**www.google.com/products**) or industry directories and listings.

Emma Henderson (profiled on page 106) saw orders flow in after a well-respected blogger spotted her collection on Etsy.com, and Paul King (profiled on page 67) says mentions on top tech sites Lifehacker and Tech Crunch was just what he needed to get his business launched in the US.

Social media marketing

Embrace social media and you can promote and distribute content, products and services far and wide. According to research company Nielsen, the world now spends over 110 billion minutes on social networks and blogs per month. This equates to 22% of all time online, or one in every four and half minutes.

66 For the first time ever, social networks or blog sites are visited by three-quarters of global consumers who go online, after the numbers of people visiting these sites increased by 24% over last year. 99

– Nielsen, June 2010

Putting this into promotional context, did you know that having a presence on just five of the biggest social networking sites gives you access to 828 million potential customers? What's even more compelling is that having a presence on these sites can be done for free. There has never before been a time when it's possible to be seen by so many, for such a small outlay.

1. Facebook

Facebook has over 500 million users accessing content and connections in more than 70 languages. You can list on Facebook for free and/or advertise on the site and select an audience based on location, age and interest.

Visit **www.facebook.com**, create an account, invite friends and contacts to join your group and get promoting.

Look my way

Ian Hendry offers four ways in which Facebook can be good for business

1. Business Pages

Facebook Business Pages enable you to set up a profile for your business which people can "like" (similar to Following on Twitter) and then they receive updates from you on their news feed and as messages. It enables you to easily add photos and video, and put updates on the business's wall and for your fans (as they used to be known) to comment and converse with you. Generate content for your Business Page by linking your blog to it so posts automatically appear on your page (supported by Posterous, **posterous.com**, and Wordpress, **wordpress.com**, add-ons to name just two) and add the Twitter application to post your tweets straight to your page. (**www.facebook.com/apps/application.php?id=2231777543**.)

 Start a Facebook business page:
www.facebook.com/pages/create.php

2. Groups
Set up groups around a common interest. If you are a physiotherapist, why not set up a group for people who enjoy running? If you're an electrical retailer, why not set up a group supporting the recycling of unwanted electrical goods? You will own the group and be able to influence its content, including promoting your business to members as appropriate.

 Set up a group on Facebook:
www.facebook.com/grouphome.php

3. Targeted advertising
Facebook has banners in the right-hand side of each page with advertisements optimised to that person's profile. You can set who you want your ads to be shown to, and can drill down to geography, age range, sex, interests, etc.

 Check out Facebook advertising:
www.facebook.com/advertising

4. Buttons
Facebook provides buttons and widgets for you to put on your own website or blog to encourage their 500 million users to share your web pages and articles with their contacts. This can be from a simple 'Find us on Facebook' button, to the 'like' buttons you see around the Facebook site itself.

 Add Facebook widgets to your website:
developers.facebook.com/plugins

Ian Hendry runs WeCanDo.biz, a sales leads and referrals network

SUCCESS STORY

Murray Newlands and Luke Brynley-Jones, Influence People

The dynamic partnership of Murray Newlands and Luke Brynley-Jones came together in 2010 to set up Influence People, a social media events company. The young start-up achieved commercial success and critical acclaim with its first conference, *Social Media Monitoring*, held in both London and San Francisco. This led to new contracts and the company is now working on a further 14 conferences in London, Paris, New York, Boston, San Francisco and Miami.

"I had already hosted two successful conferences in London," says Luke "so on the strength of those, plus Murray's credibility in the US, we were able to secure some major international sponsors. Within social media there are lots of niche industries, so it's quite easy to target specific sectors and get results, even internationally, because companies are usually delighted to hear that someone's running an event about their (often rather geeky) obsession."

Practising what they preached, Luke and Murray promoted themselves and their events through social media. They cold-emailed, wrote blog posts about companies, tweeted CEOs directly and published videos; all of which got them noticed. With staff, consultants and sponsors now based in the US, they communicate through regular Skype calls as well as Skype instant messaging and email.

"For team members we use Google Calendars (shared) and Google Docs. We also use normal phones – mainly when we're being lazy. We haven't invested in any software or communication tools because we haven't needed to. It's all free."

An international network of support is in place. They have a pair of East and West Coast 'fixers' in the US, who ensure Luke and Murray get the right partners for their events; a partner in Paris doing the same; and a US-based home-working sales team that makes calls to anywhere in the English-speaking world.

"For general marketing we are very active in social media. We have three popular blogs and over 20 active twitter accounts. We also manage three social media LinkedIn Groups and a range of Facebook pages. We sell tickets primarily through online buzz, and when that fails we use media partners, who offer discounted tickets to their members."

This fast-moving business expects a growing proportion of their work to be overseas. In 2010 they ran 10 conferences in the US and one in Paris. Events were also being planned in Barcelona and Madrid and they had invitations to work in Bombay and Hong Kong.

"We are collecting possible 'fixers' whenever we meet helpful people in different locations. In fact, we need a fixer in Spain... so if anyone reading this is interested – please get in touch!"

 www.influencepeople.com

 Luke @lbrynleyjones

 Murray @murraynewlands

Useful links

 Skype (www.skype.com)

 Google Calendars (www.google.com/calendar)

 Google Docs (docs.google.com)

Top Tip:

Social media enables anyone (literally ANYONE) to set themselves up as an expert in their field. If you genuinely know your stuff, start a LinkedIn Group about your topic and start tweeting and interacting on related blogs. It's the most cost-effective form of business networking and you can rapidly gain respect, a profile and leads. Speaking engagements really help too. Pump yourself up and get on stage as often as you can. Murray has done this so successfully at marketing events across the US that he's got his own fan club! (Luke is far too British to do anything that vulgar.)

See page 125 for more information on how to manage and communicate with a virtual team across the globe.

Fast Fact:

Facebook is the most popular social networking site in the world with 64% of all online visits in November 2009.

Source: 'Portrait of a Digital Consumer in 2010', Experian Marketing Services

2. Twitter

Twitter's global audience doubled in the space of a year (2009-10), with nearly 93 million users visiting the site in June 2010.

This micro-blogging platform looks set to keep on growing as business owners become 'twexperts' in their field and use the free tool to make connections and sell goods.

Visit www.twitter.com, create an account, start to follow friends and contacts (and their followers) and get tweeting. Users can select their language preference and Twitter now comes in French, German, Italian, Japanese and Spanish. Make the most of international Twitter apps with the advice from San Sharma and visit Twitter 101 for a guide on doing business via this social media outlet (business.twitter.com/twitter101).

5 Twitter apps to power your global business

There's a common misconception about Twitter – that it's all about what people had for lunch, or who won *X Factor*. And while there's no denying that it's great for keeping in touch with friends, it's also a powerful tool for communicating with customers and clients, wherever they are in the world.

Here are five ways to power your global business using Twitter:

1. HootSuite

If you're serious about using Twitter in your business, HootSuite is a good place to start. It's a social media dashboard from which you can manage your Twitter, Facebook and LinkedIn accounts – as used by the White House, Oxfam and Dolly Parton!

You can track the links you share on social networks and see who's clicking what and from where in the world, and manage multiple contributors, so team members can tweet on your behalf. Or, if you'd prefer, you can schedule tweets and keep in touch with your international customers while you're asleep and they're awake.

 www.hootsuite.com

2. Twitterfeed

Connect your blog to your Facebook and Twitter accounts, so that when you share a post, links are automatically shared with your networks.

If you use a blogging platform, like WordPress, you can schedule posts to appear at an optimum time for your international customers. Twitterfeed will promote your blog posts whenever they're published.

 twitterfeed.com

3. Ad.ly Analytics

Ad.ly tells you what percentage of your followers are "engaged" and how many have a low probability of viewing your tweets, what gender your followers are and where they are in the world. Use this information to understand your Twitter followers, become a better publisher or research potential new markets.

 analytics.ad.ly

4. Tweetlator

Write a tweet, as normal, and Tweetlator will translate it into 8 different languages, including French, German and Spanish. For even more options, try Tweet Translate which boasts over 40 different languages.

 www.tweetlator.com

 www.tweettranslate.com

5. SendSocial

SendSocial is perfect for sending samples of your products to your online contacts. It allows you to send a parcel, to anywhere in the world, without having a postal address.

You Tweet, Facebook or email a request to a potential customer and the recipient accepts or declines your request. SendSocial uses a delivery partner to pick up your sample and deliver it to your online contact. All the while, addresses are kept private via SendSocial's barcoding system. And you don't have to queue at the Post Office!

 www.sendsocial.com

San Sharma is community manager at Enterprise Nation (www.enterprisenation.com)

Top 20 Markets by Twitter Penetration June 2010

Total Audience, Age 15+ - Home & Work Locations*

Location	% Reach
Worldwide	7.4
Indonesia	20.8
Brazil	20.5
Venezuela	19.0
Netherlands	17.7
Japan	16.8
Philippines	14.8
Canada	13.5
Mexico	13.4
Singapore	13.3
Chile	13.2
United States	11.9
Turkey	11.0
United Kingdom	10.9
Argentina	10.5
Colombia	9.6
South Korea	9.3
Ireland	8.4
India	8.0
Malaysia	7.7
New Zealand	7.5

Source: comScore Media Metrix

*Excludes visitation from public computers such as internet cafes or access from mobile phones or PDAs.

SUCCESS STORY

Simon Burke, Ollie and Forbes

Simon and wife Gillian started Ollie and Forbes in 2008 when they came up with the idea of being a retailer of high quality toys and gifts. The products they sell are traditional with a contemporary twist.

Within six months of going live with a newly designed site, orders arrived from overseas as the couple made the most of social media to spread news about their company. Their largest export market is the US, closely followed by Australia and then Europe. Packages are sent from the local Post Office with export documentation in place and the couple use PayPal as they see this as the most secure option, readily accepted by customers across the globe.

> "Social media has most definitely been our friend. We have not paid for any direct advertising overseas. We considered exhibitions but they are expensive and with most of our international orders coming from Twitter and Facebook, which cost nothing, we're keen to continue and experiment more with social media marketing."

The company is looking to outsource fulfilment so that Simon and Gillian don't have to spend time packing boxes and they are keen to increase overseas trade, with plans to export to Asia. They will buy local sub domains for their sites and translate some of the content to see if this has an impact on sales. There's plenty of potential yet to be realised in this fast-expanding business!

 www.ollieandforbes.com

@ollieandforbes

3. LinkedIn

Referring to itself as 'the world's largest professional network', LinkedIn has 75 million members in over 200 countries. A good number of these could be your potential partners and customers. The site is available in Portuguese, English, French, German and Spanish.

Visit LinkedIn.com, create an account and start connecting with contacts and finding new ones. Form LinkedIn groups around your specialist subject or see page 93 for details on how LinkedIn can act as an effective sales platform if selling creative products. On page 92, Gerlinde Gniewosz talks about how she uses LinkedIn to find developers for her global apps business.

 www.linkedIn.com

 Fast Fact:

For the 12 weeks ending November 28 2009, visitors aged 55+ to social sites increased 77% – representing 12% of total visits.

Source: 'Portrait of a Digital Consumer in 2010', Experian Marketing Services

4. Flickr

"Share your photos. Watch the world." This is the Flickr tagline and this treasure trove of a site presents an effective way to be seen on the web. The latest data available reveals it has 40 million members (source: Yahoo, November 2009) and the extent of its international coverage is made clear by clicking on the site's world map (www.flickr.com/map).

Promote your business by uploading a combination of images and video clips that show:

➤ events you host, speak at, or attend

➤ products you make (the finished product) as well as images of the production process

➤ happy customers wearing/using/enjoying your products and services

➤ your workspace

➤ your family (if you – and they – feel comfortable showing your personal side).

Your aim here is sharing your photos and *selling* to the world. Flickr enables you to do this, and you can easily pull the photos into your blog and social media pages.

See page 88 for details of how to use image libraries as an international sales platform.

5. YouTube

YouTube is the world's most popular online video community with 24 hours of video uploaded every minute. Start your own business channel, for free, and upload videos profiling you and your work.

Create an account (www.youtube.com/create_account), start a channel (advice via YouTube video!), and start broadcasting to the world. You can give each of your videos a name and assign keywords to it to help with searching, plus you can have a short description of your company on your profile page. Again, these clips are very easy to add to your website, and they help keep the content fresh and interesting.

Measuring media

Measure which strands of social media are working best for you with these tools:

➤ ScoutLabs (www.scoutlabs.com) – measure and manage social media with this analytics tool.

✈ Tweet Reach (www.tweetreach.com) – see how far your tweets travel!

✈ Crazy Egg (www.crazyegg.com) – view the hottest topics and sections of your site.

✈ Hootsuite (www.hootsuite.com) – the social media dashboard not only helps keep social media activity in one place, it also tracks results.

Social marketing is a powerful medium, it's free and it has limitless reach, so it's worth investing the time to do it well. Spend 30 to 60 minutes each day setting up and maintaining your accounts. Cultivate a personality across your social media presence and utilise the channels to:

✈ undertake research

✈ demonstrate expertise

✈ engage with customers

✈ promote offers

✈ locate potential partners

✈ network with the world!

A warm welcome

Having invested time and effort in creating content about your subject and being found by search engines and via social media, you'll want visitors to have a good experience when they land on your site. Welcome overseas visitors by displaying written or video testimonials from residents of that country, upload any international press profile, and present tailored images and local language. See pages 130 to 132 for details on translation and the importance of having stock imagery that suits the culture of your target territory. With the website being your window to the world, be sure to keep it well polished!

How to build a business with a Small Niche and Global Reach (for less than £100)

Selling products: Let's take the example of an artisan producing handmade fashions.

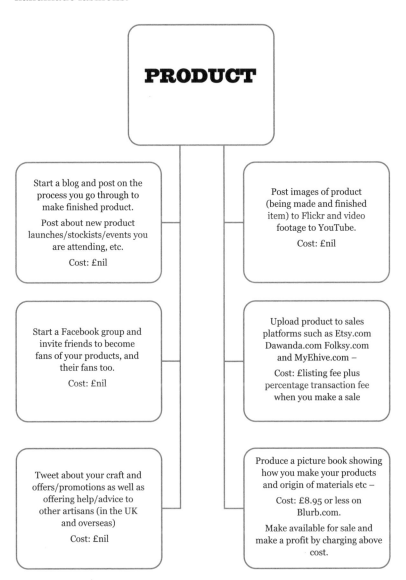

PRODUCT

Start a blog and post on the process you go through to make finished product.

Post about new product launches/stockists/events you are attending, etc.

Cost: £nil

Post images of product (being made and finished item) to Flickr and video footage to YouTube.

Cost: £nil

Start a Facebook group and invite friends to become fans of your products, and their fans too.

Cost: £nil

Upload product to sales platforms such as Etsy.com Dawanda.com Folksy.com and MyEhive.com –

Cost: £listing fee plus percentage transaction fee when you make a sale

Tweet about your craft and offers/promotions as well as offering help/advice to other artisans (in the UK and overseas)

Cost: £nil

Produce a picture book showing how you make your products and origin of materials etc –

Cost: £8.95 or less on Blurb.com.

Make available for sale and make a profit by charging above cost.

> 66 Small businesses will find opportunities to flourish in niches left untouched by the global giants. 99
>
> *Emergent Research*

Selling services: Let's take the example of a consultant, specialising in the topic of 'time management'.

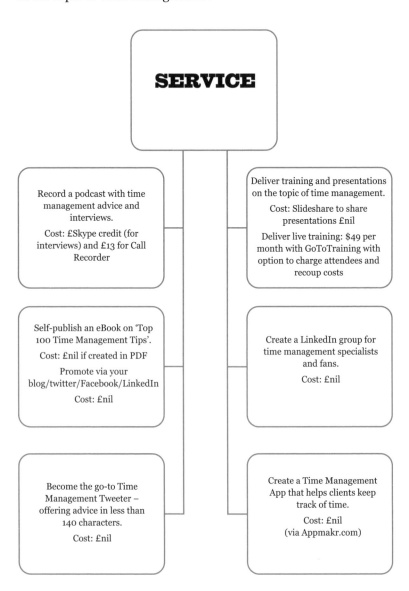

Press releases and events

The power of social media in promoting you and your business is undeniable but it's not yet time to write off (forgive the pun) the traditional press release. International press distribution services allow you to write a release, submit, pay a fee and have your news distributed to media contacts across the globe. The main service providers are:

PR Newswire – sends your release to consumers, media, bloggers, investors, analysts, opinion leaders and influencers in more than 170 countries, with the option to have your news translated into over 40 languages.

 Go Global service:
www.prnewswire.com/products-
services/distribution/global

Business Wire – offers a US service, which reaches more than 1,000 US daily newspapers, plus radio, television and online outlets. Also offers a global service, which promotes news across international networks.

 US service:
www.businesswire.com/portal/site/home/pr

 Global service:
www.businesswire.com/portal/site/home/5166

Marketwire – distributes releases based on geography, industry or speciality markets.

 Information on global packages:
www.marketwire.com/mw/include.do?pageid=534

 For a listing of international media channels including press, radio and TV visit:
www.businesswire.com/portal/site/home/distribution

"Be prepared to re-fashion your sales and business approach to fit the customs, approach and general dynamics of your chosen market. From a communications perspective, getting the right nuances is critical, as is positioning your product within the social vernacular. Anyone here in the UK who has cringed while watching a dubbed US commercial for a male hair care product will know how painful it can be when these things go wrong."

– Gordon Tempest-Hay, CEO, Blue Rubicon

Get spotted by trendwatching.com

Be seen by 160,000 business professionals in more than 180 countries by appearing in a trendwatching.com briefing. Trendwatching.com is one of the world's leading trend firms, scanning the globe for emerging consumer trends and making an appearance in one of their briefings is a sure-fire way to receive global attention. Founder Reinier Evers offers his words of advice:

"If you have come up with an innovation that is truly new, with global appeal, and is part of an emerging trend, you just email the idea, URL, and a very brief intro (mentioning which consumer trend you think the innovation is part of), and we'll ALWAYS check it out. If we like what we see, we will either cover it in a briefing, or add it to our Premium Trend Database. Easy, no?"

 www.trendwatching.com

Keeping up with the news

As well as putting yourself forward to be profiled in the international news, when doing business overseas you'll also want to keep abreast of current affairs. Here are a few go-to sources:

BBC World News – operating in English around the world (and Japanese for Japan). Its estimated weekly audience reach of 74 million makes it the BBC's biggest television service.

> "Available in more than 295 million homes, 1.7 million hotel rooms, on 81 cruise ships, 46 airlines and 35 mobile phone platforms, BBC World News broadcasts a diverse mix of authoritative international news, sport, weather, business, current affairs and documentary programming."

 www.bbcworldnews.com

Reuters – part of Thomson Reuters, it provides news and intelligence from around the globe for businesses and professionals.

 www.reuters.com

CNN International News App – delivers breaking news direct to your iPhone or iPod touch based on your chosen news stories of interest.

 www.cnn.com/mobile

Global Business show – this radio programme, presented by Peter Day, forms part of BBC World Service.

 www.bbc.co.uk/worldservice/programmes/global_business

Monocle Magazine – developed for 'an international audience hungry for information across a variety of sectors' *Monocle* magazine appears in print 10 times a year and is updated online at monocle.com. It covers international affairs, business, culture and design.

 www.monocle.com

Awards and recognition

Promote your business as part of activities that encourage global business. Contact the organisers of Global Entrepreneurship Week and tell them your story, or enter the International Trade Awards and be recognised for your success as an exporter.

 Global Entrepreneurship Week:
www.gew.org.uk

 International Trade Awards:
www.internationaltrade.co.uk/awards

Attend events

Sometimes you just can't beat meeting potential customers face to face, shaking hands and looking them in the eye. Do so by attending trade missions and shows, and speaking at events.

The British government, in the form of UK Trade & Investment, manages an active programme of trade shows, missions, seminars and 'meet the buyer' events, all of which support small businesses travelling overseas and making global sales. Sign up to receive alerts of upcoming missions, events and business opportunities – some come with financial support attached. There are two key country-visit programmes:

1. **Tradeshow Access Programme (TAP)** – provides grant support for eligible companies, and new and less experienced exporters, to exhibit overseas. In 2009-10 the programme supported more than 4,000 businesses at over 400 trade fairs, the biggest UK groups being at Paris Fashion Week and the Nuremburg Toy Fair. Individual levels of support in 2009-2010 were between £1,000 and £1,800.

 Tradeshow Access Programme:
www.ukti.gov.uk/export/accessinginternationalmarkets/
tradefairsandexhibitions.html

 Apply for support:
www.ukti.gov.uk/export/item/110682.html

2. **Market Visit Support (MVS)** – this programme provides guidance and financial support to help companies visit a market as part of a group or delegation, hosted by an international trade advisor. It is aimed at small businesses that are new to export.

Register on the national UKTI website for alerts: www.ukti.gov.uk/uktihome/register.html

For tailored advice on whether your company can claim financial support to attend missions and shows, speak with an international trade advisor in your local area. There are over 40 offices across the UK with sector specialists in each region. Locate your advisor by entering your postcode on the main Export page of the UKTI site: www.ukti.gov.uk/export

See page 151 for more information on UKTI support programmes.

Top Tip on TAP:

When applying for support from the Tradeshow Access Programme, apply ahead of making travel plans and ticket purchases or your application may be rejected on the basis you are able to make the visit within your own resources and not reliant on public support.

Plan for, and profit from, trade shows

You are signed up to attend a show and want to be sure you go well prepared and return with a full-to-bursting order book. With excerpts taken from UKTI's 'Making the Most of Exhibitions' here is an itinerary of action in the lead up to, during, and after a show, to guarantee maximum impact.

Before you go

Be clear on your objectives and what you would like to achieve.

Practicalities

➤ Set your budget, taking into account travel, accommodation and costs of exhibition requirements such as stock and/or stands. See page 145 for links to travel cost calculators.

➤ Decide on the stand area required, think about the layout and display aids and check the facilities that you need will be available on site, e.g. power supply, internet connectivity. These may need to be ordered in advance.

➤ Ensure you take a sufficient number of business cards, sales flyers or other literature in the appropriate languages. Consider whether you need the services of an interpreter.

➤ Check you have the required travel documentation; current passport, visa, travel and medical insurance and driving licence (if required). Consider arranging open return travel to allow for follow-up meetings after the event.

➤ Alert prospective customers through a pre-show email or invitation. Ideally, secure a speaking slot at the event so your presence is promoted as part of the event promotion.

➤ Make any shipping arrangements in good time and make special allowance for large and heavy exhibits which need to be on site before stand construction begins.

➤ Make a list of the items you will need with you on the stand, e.g. visitor book, pens, stapler, scissors, stationery, laptop, etc. If appropriate, be prepared to take payment at the event.

➤ It might sound extravagant, but perhaps have two of you, so that if you are busy with a customer the other can be available.

At the event

➤ Offer an incentive for people to visit your stand; a business-card prize draw is an easy way to collate people's data, and food is always popular.

➤ Ensure consistent and clear branding across the stand and in your marketing literature.

➤ You may not have time to speak to all the delegates so try to take and hand out business cards for follow up later.

➤ Wear a name badge or something that denotes you as the stand occupier.

➤ Take photos or video clips to upload to your site/blog/social media sites.

After the show

➤ On returning home, contact the people you met and follow up on opportunities identified.

➤ If there is no immediate response then keep in touch by emailing links and articles of interest and your company e-newsletter so you stay in the minds of your potential customer.

➤ If you attended a show as part of the Tradeshow Access Programme, put yourself forward to be profiled as a successful case study.

UKTI 'Making the Most of Exhibitions'
(**www.ukti.gov.uk/export/accessinginternationalmarket
s/tradefairsandexhibitions.html**)

66 Working internationally is not that different from working at home: you still need to find customers and have a compelling proposition for them to buy from you. The best advice is to make your international marketing strategy an extension of your UK strategy. 99

– Christine Losecaat, managing director Little Dipper, chair of UK China Partners

SUCCESS STORY

Raoul Tawadey, Circalit.com

It was whilst working at a film production studio as a script reader that Raoul Tawadey came up with the idea for his online business.

> "Part of my job entailed reading through the slush pile of screenplays and I realised there were hundreds of excellent scripts being overlooked because they weren't of interest to that particular producer or because they didn't tick certain boxes. That's when I realised the most effective way of showcasing talent is online, where a writer can gain more exposure through a single upload than could ever be possible printing out scripts and mailing them to agents and producers."

The company, Circalit, was launched in January 2009, and after a year in development the website followed (www.circalit.com). It has since grown to incorporate authors, publishers, playwrights and theatre companies, but the concept remains the same: connecting talented writers with industry professionals.

Around 60% of site users are from the US, but Raoul has recently seen an upsurge in users from emerging markets (the Indian user base has risen sharply) and the UK accounts for just 20% of total users.

Raoul knew from the outset that the company would have to be promoted worldwide to attract the right audience.

> "I realised that in order to get the word out there, we needed to punch above our weight and the way to do this was to form strategic partnerships with more established companies. With much of the film industry being in Los Angeles, we decided to start by partnering with UCLA film school. We followed this up by launching a joint competition with Hollywood film studio Imaginarium

Entertainment (who produced blockbusters such as *Collateral*) as well as by partnering companies in the UK and Europe like the BBC and The Script Factory."

The company has taken advantage of social media by integrating much of the site with Facebook, allowing users to share recommended scripts with their friends, and so attracting more people to the site. As the site attracts an active and niche community, Raoul has also been able to negotiate sponsorship deals with companies looking to tap into this set. And in return for exposure and advertising, Circalit has become a major sponsor of numerous film festivals and competitions, giving the company strong exposure.

At a young age, Raoul has a firm global mindset-

"We continually strive to be more global. Our market isn't geographically limited. On the contrary, we anticipate that the move towards digital distribution will facilitate a more diverse and less Hollywood-centric market for screenwriters. Over the next 12 months we're looking to have the site translated into most European and Asian languages, as well as making a strategic drive to form partnerships with top agents and producers in the Bollywood film industry."

This is an entrepreneur to watch.

 www.circalit.com

 Top Tip:

It's important that your business is solving the problem it was designed to solve before scaling up. Get the product right before embarking on overseas expansion and do the necessary research to make your product work overseas.

Top 10 promotion checklist

Check off these items to ensure all promotion angles are covered.

Action	Completed
I have worked on SEO so my site can easily be found and appears in search results when people in my target country type in the service/product I offer.	✓
I have connected with influential bloggers and popular sites in other countries and offered to post for them, and link to them.	✓
I have visited active forums and become recognised as an expert in my field through the advice I offer to others.	✓
I have a good social media presence and spend time each day keeping my profiles updated and fresh with content.	✓
When there is an important announcement to make (new product/new contract/research findings) I send a press release to an international press newswire or to local online/print/media contacts overseas.	✓
I am considering how micro-publishing, such as producing an e-book or delivering online training, could further enhance my reputation, and revenues.	✓
I have researched the potential for my company to attend international events, with funding support from UKTI.	✓
I have contacted my local trade advisor to explore opportunities for my company to be promoted via embassy and trade offices overseas.	✓
I am keeping up-to-date with news in the target country so I can respond to media opportunities as they arise.	✓
After receiving press profile overseas, I have uploaded this to my site. Having secured customers, I have uploaded their testimonials so others feel more confident in buying from me.	✓

With checks in all boxes, you'll be known across the web and have your product or service sold across the world.

SUCCESS STORY

Paul King, 1daylater.com

This business came about when Paul King was working as a freelance Sage consultant and realised he needed to keep close track of his time. With a "genius web programmer" for a brother, Paul asked David King to develop an application that would provide a solution to his time-tracking request.

The prototype was complete in March 2009, and after a year of testing the business went live. Using Google Analytics, the brothers realised that two-thirds of their customers were coming from the US, yet their website pricing was in pounds. This had to change. The product is now priced in pounds and dollars and the brothers have promoted their business in the US by encouraging American websites and bloggers to write about them. Coverage on top tech sites including Lifehacker, Tech Crunch and PC Mag has increased traffic to the site and, crucially, sales.

> "As well as pricing the product in dollars on the site, we made modifications such as recording distances in miles and kilometres and a system whereby if you regularly visit the site, the system will default to only showing prices in your local currency. Customer support happens through an online support forum so in theory we don't have to be awake through the night to respond to customer questions!"

Google Analytics is now showing the entrepreneurial brothers that they are attracting interest from Russian customers so they are researching ways to best appeal to this new market.

If Paul were to track his time now, you can guarantee a good chunk of it is being spent on international business development!

 www.1daylater.com

Useful links

> Google Analytics (www.google.com/analytics)
>
> Lifehacker (www.lifehacker.com)
>
> Tech Crunch (www.techcrunch.com)
>
> PC Mag (www.pcmag.com)

Step 3: Sell

You've done your research, have a strong profile, and are ready to make sales. Do so via your own website, through platform sites, or through agents and distributors. This section shows you how, including taking payment.

Via your own site

In our *Go Global* survey, 62% of respondents confirmed they were selling overseas via their own websites. When it comes to making sales through your own store, there are a number of options available.

Add an e-commerce plug-in to your blog

Started blogging and want to open the site up to sales? Do so by plugging in an e-commerce tool such as:

➤ WP e-Commerce shopping cart – 'suitable for selling your products, services, and or fees online' (www.wordpress.org/extend/plugins/wp-e-commerce).

➤ PayPal shortcodes – insert Paypal buttons in your posts or pages using a shortcode (www.pixline.net/2008/05/paypal-shortcodes-plugin).

➤ View a complete list of Wordpress e-commerce plugins: www.wordpress.org/extend/plugins/tags/ecommerce.

Template website with e-commerce built-in

If your site has been built using a template product, it should come with e-commerce capability built in. Companies such as Mr Site now offer a secure PayPal shop in all their website builders that start at £20 per year for the basic site plus e-commerce store (www.mrsite.com/product_comparison.asp) and platforms like Powa (www.powa.com) are designed with e-commerce in mind, allowing small-business owners to have a big-business feel for £50 per month. The technology driving the Powa platform is the same technology powering major retail sites such as Jimmy Choo, Superdrug and Monsoon.

> "Powa is dedicated to providing small businesses with affordable, easy-to-use tools and services that help them tap into their major sales channel, the web."

See page 72 to read how Quintessentially Gourmand went global with a Powa site, how the company has helped businesses in the Isle of Man take their products to the world on page 75, and how Powa can help you do the same on page 162.

In one of my other books – *Working 5 to 9: How to start a successful business in your spare time* – I offer details of companies that offer template site building packages with e-commerce capability. The list includes:

- Actinic (www.actinic.co.uk)
- Shopcreator (www.shopcreator.co.uk)
- Shopify (www.shopify.com)
- There are also open source options such as Magento which offer flexibility over the presentation, content, and functionality of your online shop. (www.magentocommerce.com)

Choose a web builder that enables you to accept multiple currencies and display in different languages. This will make your site future-ready for international trade.

'Getting British Business Online'

In 2010, the 'Getting British Business Online' project was launched by Google and Enterprise UK with a plan to offer free websites to 100,000 businesses. Project partners included Google, BT, PayPal and Enterprise UK.

www.gbbo.co.uk

Add a shopping cart to your site

Include or add a shopping cart to make life easy for your visitors to click and buy. Check out the shopping cart providers below.

✈ Groovy Cart: www.groovycart.co.uk

✈ Zen Cart: www.zen-cart.com

✈ Roman Cart: www.romancart.com

✈ OS Commerce: www.oscommerce.com

✈ Cube Cart: www.cubecart.com

✈ Frooition: www.frooition.com [shopping cart and full website]

Research the product that suits you best, taking into account hosting provision, back-end admin, and built-in search engine optimisation.

For more information on e-commerce, view the video series '10 steps to e-commerce success' produced by Enterprise Nation in association with PayPal.

✈ '10 Steps to e-commerce success':
www.enterprisenation.com/content/AudioVideo.aspx

Fast Fact:

Add a PayPal payment button to your site and you'll be able to accept payment from all major credit and debit cards, as well as bank accounts around the world. You can set it up in less than 15 minutes.

An online shop in 60 seconds

If you'd like to test the waters of global trade, website **tinypay.me** could be for you. It lets you create your shop in just 60 seconds, without even having to sign up for an account. You give a title and description to the item you'd like to sell, set your price (or how much of your price you'd like to set aside for charity) and a shop is born!

You can sell physical or virtual goods, include a few photos and add your products to a map. Tinypay.me then creates a page per product or you can embed the sale on your own website, in the same way you'd include a YouTube video.

All payments are handled by PayPal, with 5% of the total sales price going to tinypay.me. If you decide to donate a percentage to charity, tinypay.me will match you, donating the same percentage of its fee as well.

www.tinypay.me

Fast Fact:

Chinese and Korean consumers are the most prolific online shoppers in the Asia Pacific region, with 95% of internet users intending to make a web purchase in the next six months.

Source: Nielsen Online Shopping Trends 2010

SUCCESS STORY

Kenneth Benning, Quintessentially Gourmand

The model Ken Benning has decided to choose for his international expansion is a franchise one. With a background in publishing, Ken established London Fine Foods in 2003 as a group supplying high quality luxury food via the web. On behalf of customers, Ken and his team buy fine foods such as caviar, truffles, *foie gras* and other delicacies. Bearing in mind the perishable nature of such products, you may wonder how Ken is growing a global business.

"Moving goods within Europe was relatively straightforward," he says, "but I wanted to expand further afield – to North American and the Middle East. So I needed to come upon a solution."

Having approached the private members' club Quintessentially, which offers a 24-hour global concierge service via 55 franchisees, Ken launched the Quintessentially Gourmand brand, which now offers a worldwide service operating successfully via local franchisees.

"We take pleasure in finding the most exclusive and rare food products on the planet for our customers. Want to get your hands on a limited number of Kobe beef steaks as soon as they've been released from Japan? We make this possible!"

Ken is gradually introducing his fine food concept to all 55 franchisees. It presents an extra revenue stream for them and he has the security of knowing business is in good hands, with high levels of customer service available at a local level and within local time zones.

"As well as having Quintessentially as a strategic partner, our international expansion would also not have been possible without Powa.com. Utilising their e-commerce platform, we have been able to develop international sites, accepting multiple currencies. The technology is reliable which leaves me to focus on expansion and client service. We have a good deal more expansion to achieve and I'm happy that Powa will be our partner as more franchisees sign up to Quintessentially Gourmand from across the world."

www.quintessentiallygourmand.com

Sales via mobile phones

When you take into account the predicted 5 billion mobile phone subscribers by the end of 2010 (source: European Information Technology Observatory), the 60-million-plus BlackBerry devices and iPhones globally (source: EIU Digital Economy Rankings Report) and consumers in emerging markets who are increasingly using smart phones as their primary form of internet access, you soon conclude that selling via mobile platforms should be high on the list of your global considerations. According to Nielsen:

"Defying classic economic models, the demand for communication (cell phones) leads traditional media growth, signifying a global, disruptive phenomenon. The demand for information via the internet follows slower, more predictable growth patterns. The implications for marketers: lead with mobile advertising in high-growth, emerging economies."

Respond to this opportunity by creating a mobile version of your site and setting up a system to take payment. It sounds complex but you can accept mobile payments via these easy methods:

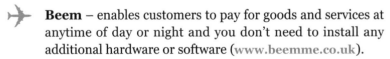

- ✈ **Beem** – enables customers to pay for goods and services at anytime of day or night and you don't need to install any additional hardware or software (**www.beemme.co.uk**).

- ✈ **Fortumo** – money is taken straight from the customer's phone bill rather than having to set up a payment account (**www.fortumo.co.uk**).

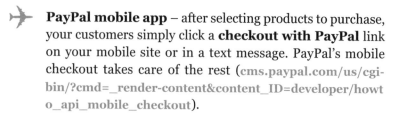

→ **PayPal mobile app** – after selecting products to purchase, your customers simply click a **checkout with PayPal** link on your mobile site or in a text message. PayPal's mobile checkout takes care of the rest (cms.paypal.com/us/cgi-bin/?cmd=_render-content&content_ID=developer/howt o_api_mobile_checkout).

→ **Waspit.com** – a simple and secure payment gateway that allows people to make and receive payments of any size to any person from a mobile phone or via the net (www.waspit.com).

❝ We have been offering mobile commerce since 2005 and our mobile transactions are growing at a dramatic rate – increasing nearly six-fold, from $25 million in 2008 to $141 million in 2009. We expect to close out 2010 with more than half a billion dollars in mobile payment volume and more than five million members regularly using PayPal from their mobile devices. ❞

– Bill Zielke, senior director, merchant services, PayPal

Data lists

For a targeted sales campaign, consider buying customer data from a data specialist such as Experian QAS or Royal Mail, bearing in mind customers are more likely to buy from you if they have given you 'permission' to promote your goods and services to them, as opposed to being approached cold.

International data from QAS:
 www.qas.co.uk/products/enhance-your-database/international-data.htm

Royal Mail data:
 www.mmc.co.uk/Campaign-masterclass/Specialist-services/International-services

Isle of Man brings in the business

In 2009, the Isle of Man Department for Economic Development launched Shop IOM, a web-based directory for local stores and an e-commerce project that aimed to address declining revenues for shop owners on the island. Over 90 local shops and suppliers are now online and selling across the world. Economic development manager Michael Alliston speaks of the benefits it has brought to business and customers.

Were the retailers that are part of Shop IOM exporting before the project began?

Before the project, a small number of local retailers were selling off-island to customers that perhaps had once lived on the island or visited and stayed loyal to a particular shop.

The project was an opportunity to offer government support to help the retail sector that was facing a number of challenges. With a growing trend of online shopping we knew that helping independent Manx Retailers go online meant helping them more ably compete in a global marketplace. The project involved the government supporting 50% of the cost of the retailer developing a website on the Powa.com platform.

Has the level of exports increased since the project began?

Yes, very much so. Products are being shipped across the world in ever increasing quantities. Manx paintings, dresses, beauty products and more are being ordered and the extra business has given a significant boost to the island's shops.

Soo Cards (www.soo-cards.com) is based in Peel and makes specialised greeting cards. Through shopiom.com they have received orders from businesses in the UK and cards with Manx themes have sold internationally, especially in Germany.

In another example, Horses and Riders (www.horsesandriders.co.uk), who sell equestrian supplies from their shop in Tynwald Mills and online, have been astounded by the level of interest in their goods from overseas. After the UK, their biggest markets are now in Finland and the USA, both of which account for substantial sales and they have sold goods as far away as Japan.

Even local services have received a boost. Euphoria Beautique (www.euphoriabeautique.com), who provide luxury spa and beauty treatments, have had orders from Spain, Canada and Australia. They can't give a pedicure to an Australian on the other side of the globe but what they have found is people with relatives living in the Isle of Man have used the site to order spa treatments for island-based relatives as birthday or Christmas presents.

For the average Manx shopper, all this success means two things. First, local shops are finding new ways to grow and flourish by bringing foreign money into the island. In turn, this should mean they can provide an increasingly varied and high-quality shopping experience in their physical stores, which are conveniently located on our doorstep. Second, it suggests local shoppers should log on to shopiom.com and take a look at exactly what it is that is making the world get their wallets out!

Michael Alliston, Department of Economic Development, Isle of Man

 ShopIOM (www.shopiom.com)

Top Tip:

When selling online, you don't want to put all your eggs in one virtual basket so consider selling on platforms, i.e. third party, sites too.

Via platform sites

Going global has never been so easy, with sites at our disposal that act as powerful and international sales platforms. All you have to do is promote your goods, services, skills and talents via these sites and they will attract global customers on your behalf – job done! Here are ten sales platforms that enable you to globally sell anything from boutique crafts to business concepts.

1. Alibaba.com

Launched by Jack Ma in China in 1999, Alibaba.com acts as a trading platform connecting buyers and sellers, suppliers and providers.

> "The privately held Alibaba Group reaches internet users in more than 240 countries and regions. The group and its subsidiaries employ in excess of 19,000 people in some 60 cities in Greater China, India, Japan, Korea, the United Kingdom and the United States."

As of March 2010, Alibaba.com had over 660,000 registered users in the UK, up 69% on the previous year. The UK accounts for 6% of all registered users on Alibaba.com's marketplace and the site added more than 22,000 new members per month in 2009.

Through the site, you can locate suppliers or make sales of your finished product direct to customers.

Alibaba.com is a champion of international trade; carrying out research on the topic, providing a platform for traders to interact, and promoting overseas sales as a form of business that is wholly viable, regardless of company size.

For more information on why you should trade on Alibaba.com, see page 158.

 www.alibaba.com

SUCCESS STORY

Marty Mannering and family, GoEco Group

Marty Mannering moved from recession-hit Middlesborough to Ireland 20 years ago to seek his fortune. He's close to achieving it by becoming the electric bike king of Ireland; selling bikes, helmets and the world's first dedicated electric bike tours. And there's an international flavour to everything he does.

Marty explains:

> "After selling electric bikes for a number of years we started to receive requests for High Nelly's; an Irish term for the old bikes used in the 50s. It was through Alibaba.com that we managed to trace a company in India that supplies parts for these bikes. We are now importing bikes from Holland, retro-fitting them in Ireland and selling electric versions of the High Nelly as well as sourcing supplies from India for parts."

Marty then recognised an opportunity in the form of bike helmets that come fashionably styled in the shape of a hat. Called 'Yakkay', Marty is importing supplies from Denmark and selling them on across the world, with 50% of orders coming from the US.

> "Having used Google Analytics to see the source of site traffic, we saw that 50% of hits on our Go Eco site were from the US and we have traffic from at least nine countries visiting our Electric Bike Holidays site. We are operating a family business in Ireland yet attracting interest and custom from across the globe and sourcing supplies from around the world. The internet has enabled this to happen and Alibaba.com has proved to be an invaluable tool for us in sourcing supplies and trade."

Marty has many more plans up his sleeve, including a High Nelly Hotel Hire Company of Ireland which he intends to export to other countries where Irish expatriates are longing for a little bit of home. He also plans to promote his business, cross border, with Northern Ireland. This global entrepreneur is certainly moving at electric speed!

 www.goeco.ie

www.electricbikeholidays.ie

 www.highnelly.ie

 www.alibaba.com

Top Tip:

Find something no one else is doing and become the best at it.

2. Amazon Marketplace

You may be used to buying from Amazon, but have you considered the site as a platform from which to sell? Have your products appear before millions of customers all around the world by signing up to Amazon Marketplace. It offers two sales options: a package for casual sellers who expect to sell less than 35 items a month (a fixed fee per sale plus a referral fee), and, for more seasoned sellers, there is the 'Sell a lot' package, which has a monthly charge plus a referral fee for unlimited sales that do not have to be in the Amazon catalogue.

 Amazon Marketplace: www.amazon.co.uk/marketplace

3. eBay

In 2010 there were 160,000 registered businesses trading on eBay in the UK, generating sales of £1.6 billion a year. Almost 90% of these businesses sold to customers outside the UK, with the top export markets being the USA, Ireland, Germany, France and Italy. Exports by British businesses on eBay generate sales of £250 million each year.

> 66 My advice to any company selling overseas on eBay is to place customer service as your top priority, make shipping costs reasonable and be able to deal with any returns. 99
>
> *– Jody Ford, Director of SMEs on eBay*

By having a store on eBay, you immediately have a global business with a ready-made international audience. Take onboard advice from successful eBay sellers Robert Pugh (page 81) and John Pemberton (page 82), who show how you can increase sales that little bit more.

 www.eBay.co.uk

 Fast Fact:

The UK's top export sales categories on eBay are:

- Vehicles and Parts
- Home and Garden
- Clothes
- Shoes and Accessories
- Sporting Goods
- Computing

eBay International Market opens up opportunities

eBay customers in Russia, the Czech Republic, Greece, Denmark, Sweden and Norway are now able to use the eBay International Market. Robert Pugh suggests sellers in the UK hoping to reach these markets should:

 offer fixed price items

 offer worldwide postage and specify postage costs

 be PayPal verified.

Since the launch of the international marketplace in early 2010, customers from these six countries have bought over five million items from overseas sellers, and the number of eBay customers in these markets has increased by nearly 200,000. Well worth making the most of these new markets and customers!

Robert Pugh is author of the weekly eBay Bulletin and *The eBay Business Handbook*

 www.ebaybulletin.blogspot.com

SUCCESS STORY

John Pemberton, Give Me Designer Clothing Global

John Pemberton has been selling through eBay for five years. During this time he has built a business with an annual turnover of more than £250,000 and monthly hits of over 50,000. John exports worldwide, with most trade in Europe, America, Canada and emerging economies, including Chile and Argentina, which John says is due to the exchange rate.

> "eBay has helped me increase sales abroad and some days I hardly post anything to the UK because the export side of my business has grown so much. My business is more recession-proof than the high street due to lower operational costs and traffic online remaining stable and I've been able to weather the UK recession as I don't rely on one single market."

The main challenge John faced has been trying to reduce shipping costs, as postage was creeping up to £10 for a £15-£20 item. But as volumes have grown, John has been eligible for better deals.

> "I never saw myself as having enough volume for Royal Mail to be interested in me, but in fact they were. I was able to qualify for a free Royal Mail pick-up (where they come to my office and pick up all the mail at a specified time). I was able to pre-print my stamps (via a system called despatch express), and the average price fell from around £7 per parcel to £3.50. This allowed me to drop my stamp prices and become more competitive.
>
> I now use a service called Royal Mail Tracked (for UK) and Contract Airsure (International). I can have a fully tracked parcel in the USA within 2-3 working days. Amazingly, countries such as Brazil and New Zealand can also use this service, so I can promote my products in new territories and ensure parcels are fully trackable.

Customers love the service and for me the costs are around 30% cheaper than using the Post Office the old way."

John says eBay has done the groundwork for him in providing the mechanism to trade. It is on the back of this platform that he's been able to build a successful and sustainable business.

✈ Give Me Designer Clothing Global:
stores.ebay.co.uk/A-Designer-Clothes-Shop

✈ Despatch Express:
**www.royalmail.com/portal/rm/content1?catId=22
700528&mediaId=22700584**

✈ Royal Mail Tracked:
**www.royalmail.com/portal/rm/jump2?catId=4000
28&mediaId=46800683**

✈ Contract Airsure:
**www.royalmail.com/portal/rm/content1?catId=40
0034&mediaId=22700566**

Top Tip:

Research each country's demand for your product and fashion your offering to appeal to that market. For example, if you sell shoes to Australia, consider providing a shoe conversion chart to make sizes clear and so there are no barriers for the customer to click the 'buy it now' button.

See page 104 for details of delivering packages to overseas customers.

International trading on eBay: a how-to guide

John Pemberton, founder of successful eBay business Give Me Designer Clothing Global, offers a crib sheet for ensuring your eBay items appeal to international markets

✈ Use eBay's 'international visibility promo upgrade'. By applying this to listings, items are visible on eBay.com, on a par with USA domestic listings.

✈ Include shipping prices for all countries, as this allows eBay to put your listings onto their new eBay.eu site, opening you up to millions more customers.

✈ Consider sometimes setting postal prices at below cost for non-EU countries to make the overall total cost appealing.

✈ Price shipping competitively, even if you lose money – look at the overall profit, not just individual elements.

✈ List some items directly on overseas eBay accounts:

✈ "I found through research that certain brands were in high demand in certain countries, so rather than let the customer search on foreign eBay sites, I listed them directly on their own domestic site, and even in their own language. This led to me sometimes having 60%+ of the whole market for that product in that respective country. One particular item was generating enough profit to actually pay my wages every month!"

✈ To research eBay prices, consider using a research tool like Terrapeak, where you can see the final (end) price for stock on eBay (UK, Germany, USA, France, etc.). Look at the demand for items in these countries and change your listings to appeal to local customers.

✈ Localise by listing in local languages using Google Translate for free, or a professional translation company.

Useful links

✈ Selling on the eBay international market: pages.ebay.co.uk/help/sell/international-site.html

✈ Terapeak: www.terapeak.com

4. Elance.com

Elance is a US-based website that assists UK professionals and freelancers in sourcing work from around the world. Whether your discipline is in IT, design or virtual administration, this site will match you with people in search of your services. Home to over 162,000 professionals, Elance is the place to turn if you have a professional or business skill to sell.

 www.elance.com

> "Sites like Yahoo Stores, Amazon, eBay and Alibaba.com offer new web-delivered services with low to no start-up costs and success-based pay-as-you-use pricing. Thanks to these e-commerce pioneers, small businesses are able to quickly setup new online businesses and start selling."
>
> – *Shipwire.com*

5. Etsy.com

This online haven for handmade artisans is an ever-growing global business, with over 400,000 sellers generating $130 million worth of goods from January to June 2010. Of this figure, 25-30% came from either a buyer or seller outside the US (which is where Etsy is headquartered). The site's top three international markets are Canada, the UK and Australia.

To ensure proximity to customers and the community Etsy has opened an office in Berlin and is launching new tools on the site, including buyers being able to see prices of goods in 21 currencies. Sellers will continue to list items in US dollars and transactions will occur in dollars, but an impending development for the site will see sellers able to list and sell in their own currency, with translation on its way too.

For anyone who makes handmade items, the power of this global platform cannot be denied.

 www.etsy.com

SUCCESS STORY

Rowena Dugdale, Red Ruby Rose

Having discovered Etsy.com in late 2007, Rowena Dugdale opened an account immediately but didn't launch her online shop selling clutch purses until the start of 2008, as she wanted time to understand the functionality of the site and experience life as a buyer. It wasn't long after Rowena's store opened that she received her first international order:

> "It took about a week – my first buyer was in Hong Kong and I was so excited! In the first few months I hardly did any promotion – customers found me through Etsy. They are still finding me through the site and 90% of my sales are to the USA, Canada and Australia. It's still a surprise to me when I receive a UK order."

With Rowena's listing price on Etsy being in US dollars, a number of her buyers don't realise she is a UK seller. This makes the working day stretch into the night on account of the time difference, with mornings being quiet and by mid-evening more communication coming in.

> "Overnight I'll have queries that I can't answer straightaway as I'm sleeping but I don't think this is a huge problem. The only other possible obstacles are shipping delays or losses, but they are fortunately rare."

Before Rowena started shipping, she made up dummy packages and took them to the Post Office to weigh so that she knew what to charge. She tries to keep shipping costs as lean as possible to remain competitive and now has digital scales and online access to postal rates, which makes things easier.

> "I ship via Royal Mail unless an overnight FedEx is required. I now have a business account and collection set up with Royal Mail, so I don't have to queue at the Post Office every day, which was becoming a bit of a chore."

Over the past two years of selling on Etsy, Rowena has picked up all she needs to know on the paperwork required for sending packages overseas. If customs forms are completed incorrectly, packages could be delayed, so checking with Post Office clerks or the courier company is recommended.

"Also, pass your financial paperwork to an accountant who can help with the currency conversions and fees involved with selling on Etsy and accepting payment through PayPal."

Rowena views the Etsy store as her US selling base and plans to have her own website by the end of the year. With the top design of Rowena's creations, you can be pretty sure she'll be selling across the world from this site too.

Top Tip:

"I found it helps to become a buyer first, to see how the transaction works from the other side. Then you can treat buyers as you'd like to be treated yourself."

– Rowena Dugdale

Red Ruby Rose on Etsy:
www.etsy.com/people/redrubyrose

Rowena's blog:
www.theredrubyrose.blogspot.com

Useful links

✈ Royal Mail Business Account:
www.royalmail.com/oba

See page 115 for guidelines on export documentation.

What would you do for a fiverr?

US website **www.fiverr.com** is the place for people to share what they're willing to do for $5. Services on offer include drawing cartoons, voice-overs and making slideshow videos. Secure global business and earn $5 a time via this site!

6. iStockphoto

Want to sell your photography, illustrations, videos or music effects around the world? This is the site for you:

> "iStockphoto is the web's original source for royalty-free stock images, media and design elements. For over 10 years artists, designers and photographers from all over the world have come here to create, work and learn."

To start selling, all you have to do is join the site, apply to be a contributor and submit samples of your work. As a contributor, you receive a base royalty rate of 20% for each file downloaded, which goes up to 40% if you exclusively display work on the site.

 www.istockphoto.com

A picture of profitability

For photographers, whether part-time or full-time, amateur or professional, research these top four sites, recommended by Lee Torrens, as a route to making sales.

- iStockphoto.com: **www.istockphoto.com**
- Shutterstock.com: **www.shutterstock.com**
- Dreamstime: **www.dreamstime.com**
- Fotolia: **www.fotolia.com**

Lee Torrens is the author of Microstock Diaries **(www.microstockdiaries.com)**

SUCCESS STORY

Lee Torrens, Microstock Diaries blog

Lee Torrens is probably the world's leading expert on Microstock, the name given to the royalty-free stock photography market that operates exclusively online, sourcing photos from the public. He has developed this reputation on the back of utilising social media to its full extent. He is a fine example of someone who has achieved success by developing a niche and promoting this to a global audience. It all happens from a base in Argentina:

> "My core income comes from the blog, which generates revenue from direct advertising and affiliate programs. The blog has also brought me a surprising number of other opportunities; I've done some consulting, market research and worked on conferences by setting the topics and hosting the event. I licence my own photos but haven't shot any new content for two years, so it accounts for progressively less of my income. We've just developed a Microstock plug-in (**www.microstockplugin.com**) but this is not yet profitable so can't be considered an income stream. The same is true for Microstock Charts (**www.microstockcharts.com**). These two projects provide more non-monetary benefits, such as appreciation in the marketplace and additional contacts."

Everything Lee does is global from the outset. His blog is online, so available from everywhere, with readers predominantly coming from the countries in which stock photography is a bigger industry. Advertisers are well spread out, with clients in Canada, The Czech Republic, Norway, Russia and the US. With photos licensed by online agencies, they are also sold into all parts of the world.

> "Blogging is my main promotion tool. By establishing a blog early, creating lots of useful content, and always keeping my readers' needs in mind, my blog has become

very successful in the industry. All my opportunities stem from that central resource, which I continue to build enthusiastically. I use mailing lists and a few select social media sites (Twitter, LinkedIn and Facebook) as outposts, directing traffic back to the blog."

Being an Australian and married to an Argentinean, Lee has built a business that gives him geographic freedom; doing things online makes this achievable.

"When my wife and I met I was working in a regular job for a regular company, wearing a suit to the office every day. I knew geographical freedom would be very helpful when married to someone from another country. I started a web development business and everything else flowed from there. Geographical freedom also makes it easy for me to continue my regular business when I'm travelling to industry events and it allows me to work from home and save on the costs of an office. There are many advantages to this way of working."

Lee's plans for the next year involve consolidating the business and building on his reputation as an expert in his field. From a home office, he shows how it is possible to build several revenue streams from one niche and generate income from various geographies.

 www.microstockdiaries.com

@microstock

7. iTunes

Are you a creator of audiobooks, publisher of podcasts or developer of apps? Then the iTunes platform is your channel to the global market. For apps, Apple gives 70% of revenues from the App store instantly to the seller, and they retain 30%. As of September 2010, there were over 250,000 apps and 6.5 billion downloads, making the App Store the world's largest mobile application platform. Become a registered Apple developer for the iPhone (developer.apple.com/iphone), submit audio books to iTunes via Audible.com (www.audible.com) and create iBooks for the iPad through the iBookstore. Apple is opening up a world of opportunity for content creators and app developers.

   www.apple.com/itunes

iTunes and VAT

VAT is charged at the rate payable in the country in which the sale is made. When selling via the iTunes platform, you should charge VAT on sales within the UK and EU. There is no way of charging VAT on top of the iTunes sales price, so any tax comes out of the listed sales price.

SUCCESS STORY

Gerlinde Gniewosz, Zuztertu

Gerlinde Gniewosz fell in love with the idea of mobile applications when she first set eyes on the iPhone. Not only were apps being bought in their millions, you could create them yourself without the need for expensive equipment or costly distribution. To test the market Gerlinde created a geography quiz. It sold well so she decided to develop more apps, and her company now has a portfolio of over 50 applications providing mobile education on the move.

> "Designing for mobiles is fundamentally different to designing for the web – both in terms of the user interface and the technical constraints. The combination of good design sense and technical skills is not that easy to find. However, I have managed to gather a good pool of developers and designers through online freelance portals, LinkedIn and word of mouth."

Gerlinde may be the only employee of her business but at any one time she is orchestrating an international team of 10-15 people. She uses email and Skype to keep in touch, and online project management tools so that all team members are up-to-date on each project's status.

Not only does Gerlinde work with an international team, she sells to an international marketplace through iTunes. With apps ranging from German verb tables, to a Cuban music course and a London Museum Guide written in Russian, Gerlinde maintains an international flair throughout her thriving business.

 www.zuztertu.com

@zuztertu

8. LinkedIn

LinkedIn is the world's largest professional network, with over 70 million members in over 200 countries. A new member joins LinkedIn approximately every second, and about half of all members are outside the US. As well as a medium to promote your business, it's also now possible to secure sales through it with the newly launched Creative Portfolio Display application. This aims "to empower creative professionals by creating a one-stop solution for maintaining their work portfolio and broadcasting it to millions".

LinkedIn Creative Portfolio Display:
linkd.in/deDVX1

Introducing Bitsy to the world

If you are a provider of business and professional services, then upload your profile to Bitsy and start trading with local businesses, before making the move overseas. Bitsy is a new website from the team at Enterprise Nation. It connects buyers and sellers of business services and we are practising what we preach in this book in planning to send the site global!

● **www.bitsythis.com**

    @BitsyTalk

9. oDesk.com

This site was developed to meet the needs of companies who want to employ a global workforce. According to CEO Gary Swart, oDesk was designed with global reach in mind:

> "We recognised globalisation was in full swing, the internet was continuing to grow and economic conditions meant companies wanted to get jobs done but maybe couldn't afford to employ people full time, or from their host country. oDesk.com was launched in response to these factors. What we offer is an online global employment platform that helps companies hire, manage, and pay a flexible workforce."

What this means for British business is you can access oDesk.com to hire a team of experts or, as an expert yourself, source work from around the world.

 www.odesk.com

Tips from the top

oDesk CEO Gary Swart offers advice on how best to secure work on oDesk.com

1. *Create a great profile* that offers a complete picture of who you are and differentiates you from others. Polish this off with a professional cover letter.

2. *Take certification* – oDesk.com offers over 300 certifications, which inspire confidence in the customer that you have the skills for their job.

3. *Be flexible at the start* – be prepared to accept lower fees at the outset to secure work, show you can perform, and build relationships. As your credibility on the site grows, so do the chances of being able to increase your rate.

4. *Work at managing the virtual relationship* – oDesk.com helps this happen with a desktop app that makes it feel almost as if you're working in the same office.

5. *Deliver* what you said you would!

---

10. Ooh.com

Ooh.com is a listings site for activities, courses, classes and events anywhere in the world. Use the site to sell activities at a fixed time and fixed price. Free to use for buyers and sellers, the site launched early in 2010 and already has a listing of 3,000-plus courses and activities.

 www.ooh.com

@oohdotcom

Trading in translation

If you are a linguist looking for work across the globe, there are sites on which to display your skills and source work:

- Lingo24 (**www.lingo24.com**)
- Proz (**www.proz.com**)
- Language 123 (**www.language123.com**)

See page 130 for information on the benefits of hiring translators to have your website localised.

Agents and distributors

Another route to making sales is through an agent or distributor.

An agent acts as your representative on the ground, secures sales on your behalf and is usually paid in the form of a commission per sale. It is advisable to have an agreement in place so that both parties have shared expectations and agreed targets from the outset.

For more details, view the Business Link guide on using an overseas agent: bit.ly/a786XR

An arrangement with a distributor involves a company or individual buying from you, and them selling on the goods or service at a higher price in their local market. This form of business may also be referred to as wholesaling.

> 66 A distributor takes ownership of the goods and therefore can do with them as they wish, which means you must trust them with your brand. It is always worth spending time ensuring the relationship is documented and well thought through. 99
>
> – *Business Link guide on using an overseas distributor*

At what cost?

Make sure your pricing makes you a profit, taking into account any modifications that may need to be made to suit the local market, the costs of transportation, and any local sales taxes. See page 117 for details on how to check on local duties or taxes that may apply. International trade advisors and the business trade bodies listed on page 237 will also be able to offer advice.

SUCCESS STORY

Janan Leo, CocoRose London

Selling delicate and well-designed ballerina pumps is Janan Leo's trade, and approximately 40% of her business now comes from overseas. At home, sales are made to top stores including Fortnum & Mason, and abroad CocoRose London's products are stocked in high-end boutiques from Milan to Sydney.

Janan's export journey began when her products were spotted in a London boutique by a Japanese and then Italian distributor.

"Since then, we've had quite a journey and very quickly realised there is a huge demand for British design abroad. Working with our distributors has been a steep learning curve, as we had never done this before and we are still learning everyday! Italy is our top selling export market and in terms of stockists, we would not have known where to start. However, with our distributor, CocoRose London now has a presence in approximately 50 mid- to high-end boutiques and we have an active PR campaign with an Italian PR company."

Products are currently made in China where Janan spends up to three months each year with her suppliers and manufacturing partners, forging strong relations and ensuring brand standards are met. Whilst there, Janan is also able to source materials and work on new concepts and designs for CocoRose London's forthcoming collections.

With customers all over the world, the company set up an account with currency exchange broker, First Rate FX, so they could easily make and accept payment in multiple currencies. Following a meeting with the UK Trade & Investment team, CocoRose London uncovered potential support in opening up new markets for export that they hope will mirror their Italian success.

"The potential and opportunities to be had with exporting are immense. The paperwork can initially be a bit daunting but once you start, you realise it's not as complicated as it can be made to appear. If you've got a good opportunity, seize it!"

 www.cocoroselondon.com

@cocorose

 First Rate FX (www.firstratefx.com)

 UK Trade & Investment (www.ukti.gov.uk)

Top Tip:

"When managing a manufacturing base overseas, build as much time into your plan as you can. Remember, in the early days you may be lower down the pecking order and particularly when dealing with Asia the cultural differences in doing business will lengthen the time it takes to get designs made and delivered to the UK. Oh, and make the most of all the contacts you know and who could help!"

SUCCESS STORY

Louise Unger, The Camouflage Company

Louise Unger and her sister, Corinne Laurie, had been trading for two years when they heard from their first overseas customer in search of their camouflaged garden covers. This particular customer was French superstore, Carrefour.

"We had met the buyers at the Trade Fair Glee in Birmingham," says Louise. "They liked what they saw and, as you can imagine, we were pretty delighted when they got in touch to place an order!"

Seeing there was a clear market for their products in France, Louise and Corinne then went one step further and, having attended a French trade show, Maison et Objets, they met a distributor whom they appointed for the French market. The relationship is working well and the company handles business development and shipping for them.

"We expected the export documentation process to be a challenge but it hasn't been at all. And having a positive experience in France has encouraged us to look at ways of increasing our international sales."

The company has customers in Germany and a customer in South Africa who is now interested in distributing Camouflage products there. The entrepreneurial sisters are about to spread their camouflaged wings across the globe.

 www.thecamouflagecompany.com

 @camouflageco

 Glee trade show (www.gleebirmingham.com)

 Maison et Objet trade show (www.maison-objet.com)

Accepting payment

According to a European Commission report ('E-commerce in Europe') involving 11,000 test orders of 100 popular products, 60% of potential European internet shopping orders do not go ahead because of store owners failing to offer shipping to the customer's country, or owing to inadequate means for cross-border payment.

> 66 The study underlines the importance of thinking local in e-commerce. It is vital to have your customers choose how they want to pay by offering the right and sufficient payment methods and currencies. 99
>
> – *Ogone Payment Services*

Following on from this research came a further survey that brought to light a number of UK businesses with European trading aspirations but without the payment systems in place to support such customers.

> 66 According to our survey, western European online retail sales are projected to grow 11% to reach £153 billion by 2014. However, when questioned, 79% of directors felt their payment systems were not ready. 99
>
> – *Shane Fitzpatrick, Chase Paymentech Europe Limited*

So it's important you give visitors to your site every reason to complete their purchase by having a payment system that is geared up for international trade and recognised as stable and secure. In the Enterprise Nation *Go Global* survey, respondents revealed they used the following methods:

 online payment gateway: 65%

 cheques and direct payment into business bank account: 24%

 foreign currency broker: 3%.

Online payment gateways

PayPal

Regarded as the leading international payment platform, PayPal has more than 84 million active registered accounts (nearly 220 million accounts in total) and is available in 190 markets.

PayPal supports payments in 24 currencies and has localised websites in 20 markets including Australia, Canada, China, France, Germany, the UK and the United States. For online store owners, PayPal is easy to introduce and offers customers peace of mind that payment will be secure. The company offers three main products: 'website payments standard', 'website payments pro' and 'express checkout'.

To enable your customers to buy multiple items, use a free PayPal shopping cart. To put the 'Add to Cart' button on your website with HTML code you can simply copy and paste from PayPal to the coding of your own site. Your customers then click the button to make a purchase.

 Add PayPal button:
bit.ly/blxrUn

With PayPal, there are no set-up charges, monthly fees or cancellation charges, and fee levels vary depending on the volume of sales. See page 160 for more details on pricing and an overview of how PayPal can help your business go global.

 www.paypal.co.uk

Fast Fact:

PayPal's Total Payment Volume in 2009 represented nearly 15% of global e-commerce and 16.5% of US e-commerce.

RBS Worldpay

With its main product 'Business Gateway Plus', RBS Worldpay helps over half a million businesses accept a wide range of payments in multiple currencies. There is a set-up fee of £75, a monthly fee of £15 and a charge of 3.35% per transaction plus 15p per transaction.

 www.rbsworldpay.com

"When trading overseas, treat PayPal as your friend."

– *Colin Shelbourn, cartoonist and exporter*

Google Checkout

Google Checkout is a global payment system. There are no set-up charges and fees depend on the volume of your sales. With monthly sales of less than $3,000, the fee is currently 2.9% plus $0.30 per transaction. This transaction fee decreases in line with sales volumes increasing.

 checkout.google.com

Moneybookers

Moneybookers enables small business owners who are trading overseas to accept a range of payment options, including credit cards, domestic and international bank transfers, and cheques. Signing up for a business account is quick to do. You choose the payment option to accept payments and then create Moneybookers payment buttons to appear on your site. Fees charged depend on sales volume, starting at 2.9% plus €0.29 for sales value of 0-1,000 euro. A full list of fees is available at:

 www.moneybookers.com/app/help.pl?s=m_fees

www.moneybookers.com

Sagepay

Sage Pay Go is a card payment service that allows you to accept payments by PayPal and major debit and credit cards. It is simple to manage and easy to integrate within your website. The fee is £20 per month for merchants processing up to 1,000 transactions per quarter and 10p per transaction for merchants processing more than 1,000 transactions per quarter, with a minimum charge of £20 per month. There are no set-up fees, no percentage fees and no annual charges.

 www.sagepay.com

Currency converter

Know how many dollars you're earning or how many euros you're spending with online currency converter **www.xe.com**.

See pages 170 to 222 for a list of local currencies in the UK's top 30 export countries.

Business banks

Your bank will offer an international trade service, but shop around and visit the major banks' sites to view products on offer and fees that apply.

✈ HSBC:
   www.hsbc.co.uk/1/2/business/international/services

✈ Lloyds TSB:
   www.lloydstsbbusiness.com/internationalservices/index.asp

✈ NatWest:
   www.natwest.com/commercial/international.ashx

✈ Barclays:
   www.barclays.co.uk/Internationalbankingservices/P12425
   59989153

These banks also offer advice on doing business overseas in the form of country reports, guidance on documentation and country or sector-specific events.

Foreign currency brokers

When trade volumes justify the move, consider opening a foreign exchange account with a currency broker. They act on your behalf to ensure you get the best exchange rates. Providers include:

✈ Interchangefx (www.interchangefx.co.uk)

✈ First Rate FX (www.firstratefx.com)

✈ Globex Foreign Exchange Corporation (www.globexfx.com)

* * *

Sales are coming in via your own and third party sites and payments are being safely received. The business is looking in good international shape. The next step is delivering on it.

Step 4: Deliver

This step is all about delivering on what you have promised; delivering goods, doing so in a way that meets with documentation and regulatory requirements, and with a level of service that will ensure customers keep coming back.

Let's start with how to get goods from country A to country B.

Shipping and postage

This section is of relevance to companies producing physical products. When selling services, these, in the main, can be delivered online via email, PDF documents, and other distribution channels referenced on page 56, so questions of packaging, weight and customs documentation rarely apply. Do remember the VAT, though, as that does still apply!

But what happens when you need to send a package of products to a customer in Paris? There are a number of companies vying for your business and making promises of safe, rapid and cost-efficient delivery. For small items, consider Royal Mail.

Royal Mail

A significant 85% of respondents to the *Go Global* survey said they post and deliver their goods via the local Post Office and Royal Mail. Here are the products and support on offer for businesses sending packages and parcels that are small in size.

- ✈ **International Business Airmail** – this is the most cost-effective way to send mail worldwide. It takes 3-7 working days and costs from 60p.

- ✈ **Airsure** – a fully tracked service to 30 destinations worldwide. It takes 2-6 working days and is Airmail price plus £4.90.

- ✈ **International Signed For** – provides extra reassurance that your item has been delivered, takes 3-7 working days and costs Airmail price plus £4.25.

The Royal Mail website is a useful source of information, not only on the Group's international product line-up but also covering topics ranging from sourcing data on international customers to producing country reports.

Useful links

 Landing page for International Business Customers:
bit.ly/d2A88K

Royal Mail International delivery options:
bit.ly/1sDMOe

> "There's not a single country on the planet we don't reach."
> – *Royal Mail*

International mail checklist

Follow this checklist and advice from Royal Mail and it will help get your mail to its destination as quickly as possible:

Address your mail fully and clearly and always include the zip code or postcode and the country in English. The country must be written on the last line of the address in CAPITALS.

Check you're using the correct tariff for the country you're posting to as underpayment can cause delays. View current prices at bit.ly/NoYub.

Check the minimum and maximum size limits as well as weight limits for the country you're sending to before posting. View size and weight restrictions at bit.ly/atAHJX.

If you're sending a packet outside the EU, you must complete a customs declaration for each item. Any item with contents up to the value of £270 should have a CN22 declaration attached to the front. Any item sent with a value in excess of £270 needs a fully completed CN23 declaration. Both forms are available from the local Post Office or you can download at bit.ly/cfDJZJ.

 Packaging material should protect the items enclosed from damage and be fastened securely to avoid them coming undone in transit.

Source: Royal Mail International Mail Checklist (bit.ly/ckraFp).

SUCCESS STORY

Emma Henderson, Showpony

After graduating from the Glasgow School of Art, Emma Henderson applied her talent for screen printing and launched Showpony in 2006. Working from her spare room in a Glasgow apartment, she would import fair trade bags from India, apply her unique designs, and sell the finished products at local craft fairs. It was after opening a store on handmade site Etsy.com that she quickly started to receive orders from America. Before she even had time to officially register the company, Emma was making sales across the Atlantic.

> "In the beginning a lot of it was guess work. I didn't know about export documents and shipping but with help from the staff in my local Post Office and some words of wisdom from the UPS delivery man, I got to know how it works!"

Emma's products on Etsy were soon spotted by a journalist and a feature in the US edition of *Country Living* led to increased sales. This gave her the confidence to head to New York and exhibit at Design Boom, where she met many more customers and a distributor. Unable to access public support or grants, Emma used her dad's Airmiles, but the trip was worth it, leading to a commission for Urban Outfitters and sales to major stores including Anthropologie.

The company also now has a distributor in Japan and is selling to France, Spain and Finland, receiving payments via PayPal and keeping customers happy by using a next-day delivery service.

After two years of research, Emma has found a new factory in India that makes her bags and she's moved out of the spare room into a studio with dedicated screen-print space.

"My advice to anyone considering international trade is just to be open to the opportunity and get to know the influential bloggers in that territory. Being known online is what leads to sales. My plan is most definitely to increase the countries to which I sell and if I can get a holiday out of it, then even better!"

 www.showpony.co.uk

@showpony_design

Couriers

If you have higher volumes and larger packages, consider the services of international courier companies. Here are five options, followed by a listing of price-comparison sites, and a little price comparison of our own.

1. **DHL** – Started in 1969, they were the first door-to-door international express delivery service. 40 years on, they deliver to more than 120,000 destinations in 225 countries. "We're a

walking GPS," says a company representative, "locals stop our drivers for directions. We're at home anywhere in the world, and that matters to anyone with overseas shipping needs."

 www.dhl.co.uk

2. **UPS** – Offering a range of options, from same-day services to express worldwide, this company is the largest express carrier and package delivery company in the world.

 www.ups.com

International trade services at bit.ly/b7roff.

 Fast Fact:

In a survey conducted by PayPal and comScore, 43% of shoppers said they abandon their shopping carts because of unexpectedly high shipping charges.

Source: Shipwire.com

3. **FedEx** – Offers a number of international services as well as hosting regular trade promotion events around the world linking businesses to new export markets. The company has intra-European and intercontinental services with varying guarantees on timing of delivery.

 FedEx small business centre at at.fedex.com/9xzx3I.

 Fast Fact:

There are 200 aircraft movements each night in and out of the FedEx Memphis hub. Over 15,000 employees sort up to 500,000 packages an hour and 1.5 million packages each night with the help of 300 miles of conveyor belt.

4. **Parcelforce Worldwide** – Part of the Royal Mail Group, Parcelforce Worldwide offers guaranteed express deliveries covering 99.6% of the world's population. Two key services offered are 'Express', with next-day delivery and tracking, and 'Scheduled', which guarantees delivery in three working days to Europe and US, and in four working days to most other destinations.

 www.parcelforce.com

Search the international directory to view details of the country to which you are exporting: bit.ly/bUG6RH.

> "As my products are small I offer free worldwide postage and charge one price for all of my kits – it makes overseas buyers happy to purchase from me as they know the items will not cost them more."
>
> *– Holly Hinton, Holly's Hobbies*
>
> *www.hollyshobbies.co.uk*

5. **TNT Express** – Established in the UK in 1978, TNT offers a global express, logistics and international mail service, assisting companies with their worldwide orders and delivering in excess of 100 million items per year.

 www.tnt.com

Comparing prices

As well as the courier companies, there are online destinations where you can compare international shipping prices and services. Sites include:

 Parcel2go.com: www.parcel2go.com

 Parcel2ship: www.parcel2ship.co.uk

 Parcelmonkey.com: www.parcelmonkey.com

Our own go compare

Price comparison for a package weighing 2kg and measuring 12cm by 12cm being collected from Shrewsbury, Shropshire, and delivered to the Chrysler Building, New York:

Courier	Cost
DHL www.dhl.co.uk	DHL Express Worldwide, takes 1-2 days £58.80
FedEx www.fedex.com	FedEx International Economy £60.95
Parcelforce Worldwide www.parcelforce.com	Global Economy package takes 28 days delivery and is not tracked £34.19 Or Global Express takes 1 day delivery and is tracked £58.99
TNT www.tnt.co.uk	Global Express £107.42
UPS www.ups.com	UPS Express Saver – parcel arrives by end of next working day £59.82
Using www.parcel2go.com	FedEx World Express: £34.54 [3 days] Parcel2GoExpress £42.40 [3 days] DHL Worldwide Express £24.13 [4 days] FedEx World Economy £32.00 [5 days]

SUCCESS STORY

Jane Field, Jonny's Sister

It was sending one of her personalised cushions to the editor of *Country Living* that really started things moving for Jane Field. With the magazine having a fan base of Australian readers looking for British-made goods, orders started to roll in.

"At the beginning our international sales were 2-3% of total sales. That has now increased to 15-18%, with no extra marketing effort. In fact, it would be frightening to think of the international sales we could achieve if I had the time to promote us overseas. Through word of mouth, we have become well known in expatriate communities around the world and I can only just keep up with the orders coming in, so there's little time left to court new ones."

Jane receives regular orders from Bermuda and Barbados and has a growing customer base in the US, to whose emails she responds at around 11pm "as I think it's good customer service to respond as fast as you can."

The company supplies to shops in Singapore, has a trade customer in Athens and is kept busy by mail order companies in Sweden, Denmark and Germany. Parcels of individual items are insured and delivered by Royal Mail. Jane has found this the most cost-effective option and it means she's able to track the progress of larger shipments. Her international success has been achieved without any support from trade schemes or programmes.

"Exporting sounds like a big deal but if you take it bit by bit, you soon realise it's perfectly possible, whatever the size of your company."

Not only are the products heading to international destinations, Jane is too as she is travelling to Peru to meet with the Peruvian government and explore the potential of manufacturing there.

Time permitting, she'd like to exhibit at the New York Gift Fair, promote the company in new territories with high expat populations and have parts of her site translated. But there are only 24 hours in a day and this busy lady is already filling most of them.

 www.jonnyssister.co.uk

@jonnyssister

Local shipping

As sales volumes grow, consider the benefits to your business of local shipping: this is the process whereby your products are stored overseas, typically in the country of the customer, making it easier to store and ship goods and reducing the cost for the end customer. Fulfilment is offered by a local third-party provider – usually a logistics or fulfilment service that will provide both storage and shipment.

Online buyers want their purchases fast and with the lowest possible shipping rates. Local shipping allows you to accomplish both.

66 When local customs around the world can hold packages for literally weeks on end, storing merchandise in a foreign market is the missing link that eliminates the hassles, cost and time constraints associated with shipping internationally. 99

– Source: Shipwire

The benefits of selling globally and shipping locally include:

➤ Saving on shipping costs and reduced shipping time. Local shipping rates can cut days or weeks off shipping time and up to 75% off costs.

➤ The ease of having inventory in one warehouse if a high level of sales are in one region of a country or products are perishable.

➤ The ability to process local returns.

➤ The ability to open up new sales channels such as local eBay, Amazon or local drop shippers.

➤ Offering fast and free local shipping promotions which can lead to increased sales.

➤ Outsourcing fulfilment and storage to local providers means you benefit from having a similar infrastructure to global corporations who have warehouses across the world, but you only pay a fraction of the cost.

See page 128 for more information on how to 'go local' in international markets.

Over the ocean waves

To view a guide on how to transport goods by sea, visit the Business Link guide: **bit.ly/aLM9ss**

How to grow your e-commerce business through outsourced fulfilment

Nate Gilmore, vice president at Shipwire, offers guidance on the benefits of having a global warehousing network and what to look for when choosing a partner.

Many entrepreneurs start out by selling a product online in a marketplace like eBay or via their own online store, and ship to buyers right out of the garage or spare room. This is a fantastic way to start a business but it can make for long nights and weekends as sales start to ramp up. With today's global marketplace, buyers will be finding you from around the world, so as a seller you'll be navigating shipping and customs needs. If you're asking yourself when you can get back to working on the business, then outsourcing order fulfilment and local shipping might be your answer.

Outsourced order fulfilment
Outsourced storage and shipping goes by several names: outsourced order fulfilment, third-party fulfilment, 3PL or third-party logistics, outsourced shipping, warehouse distribution service or product fulfilment. It all means the same thing, finding a warehouse service company to store your physical inventory. When outsourcing order fulfilment, you receive orders and send them out to a partner warehouse, where items are picked, packed and shipped on to the buyers.

The most important part of outsourcing order fulfilment is finding a trusted partner. When vetting partners, bear these factors in mind:

 Try before you buy – get a free trial and do an 'end-to-end test' by sending the vendor sample inventory and routing it back to yourself. If this is an overseas warehouse, send a sample to a friend local to the market or talk to your first few customers and get their feedback on the shipment process and maybe some pictures of the boxes and labels.

 Seek transparent pricing – avoid long-term agreements and hidden costs like volume commitments.

Invest in growth markets – do your research. Look at past sales and check online at local product prices and past sales history in the local market. Then look for a global warehouse network with warehouses in your growth markets.

 Connect via software – look for a software platform you can easily plug into your website or other sales channels. Make sure your orders are automated to the warehouse and there is an automated returns process. As overseas warehouse customer support hours may be your sleeping hours, the system needs to be automated so you can rest easy.

Outsourcing fulfilment enables you to handle increased sales volume without having to build your own warehouse and you are in control of costs should sales decrease.

Nate Gilmore is a vice president at Shipwire, a provider of outsourced e-commerce product fulfilment with warehouses in the UK, United States and Canada. Nate posts about global trade and local shipping at www.shipwire.com/blog.

Administration

Your product is about to be shipped to your customer or to the third-party fulfilment provider. Do you have insurance in place and the right documents completed? It's time to deliver according to trading rules and regulations.

Export documentation

Exporting brings with it a duty to inform HM Revenue & Customs here in the UK, and the customs authority in the host country to which parcels are being sent.

As outlined on page 106, when posting packets or parcels outside of the EU you will need to complete a CN22 or CN23 declaration.

Any item with contents up to the value of £270 must have a current CN22 declaration attached to the front. You should sign and date the form. They are available at Post Offices, via your courier company or online download at: bit.ly/bpmEsm

Any item sent with a value in excess of £270 must have a fully completed CN23 declaration. They are available at Post Offices, via your courier company or online download at: bit.ly/bEseif

See page 227 for copies of these declarations. Correct completion will ensure your package makes it past customs in the receiving country. You do not need a customs declaration for packages sent to another country within the EU, with the exception of those countries mentioned in the boxout here.

These countries are in the EU but you will still need to complete a customs declaration when sending items:

Channel Islands – Jersey, Guernsey, Alderney, Herm and Sark

Andorra

Canary Islands

Gibraltar

San Marino

Vatican City State

Proof of export

If you are a VAT-registered business supplying items that are zero-rated (i.e. no VAT applies) overseas and via the Post Office, you are required to present customs with proof of export. This is through 'A Certificate of Posting' which can be obtained at your local Post Office or downloaded at: bit.ly/b5Xlxc

The certificate must be signed and date-stamped by a member of Post Office staff in order to be valid.

Tax treatment of exports

In most cases, exports will be zero-rated for VAT although there are exceptions. Call the HMRC VAT Helpline on 0845 010 9000 for advice on your particular product or service.

For VAT-registered businesses, details of exports you make should be included on your VAT return. If you have a high level of exports to European Union member states, you may have to offer more details in monthly Intrastat declarations. This applies if your purchases from EU member states total more than £600,000 of goods, and/or your sales to EU member states will reach £250,000 in a year. This is for companies producing goods and does not apply to service-based businesses.

 Download Intrastat returns on the Business Link website: bit.ly/dss88P

If the goods are leaving the European Union you won't need to include VAT on your international invoices.

With regard to corporation tax, if you are making sales from a UK-based business with no presence overseas, you will not be liable to pay corporation tax in the country to which you are exporting.

Commodity code

When completing customs declarations for exports outside the EU, a customs commodity code is required that describes the nature of your product. Use the UK trade tariff to find the appropriate code:
www.businesslink.gov.uk/bdotg/action/tariff

Exporting legalities

When you export goods to other countries, they become subject to that country's laws. Speak to an international trade advisor (locate your local contact as per guidance on page 153), or consult with the trade bodies listed on page 223 with regard to any compliance with local laws and regulations.

With regard to export licences, it is unlikely you will need one unless you are supplying goods such as military or paramilitary goods, artworks, plants and animals, medicines and chemicals.

Definitions

Movements of goods between EU member states are called 'arrivals' (acquisitions, purchases or imports), and 'dispatches' (removals, sales or exports).

The national export system

For exports outside the EU and sent *via freight*, sales must be reported to HMRC electronically using the national export system (NES) or by completing the paper-based single administrative document (SAD). This is not relevant for exports sent by post.

66 The National Export System is an electronic processing system through which all export declarations to third countries are processed. **99**

– Overview of the national export system (bit.ly/aarI75)

 To access the NES online and input details visit: bit.ly/9Pf3S4

 Download the single administrative document via the HMRC website: bit.ly/cVzRyw

Intellectual property

Intellectual property of your product or service is based in the territory in which it is delivered. What this means is if you have protected your intellectual property in the UK, the protection may not apply outside the UK. Certain countries will extend your UK protection, after completing local requirements. To find out more on registering trademarks and patents, or protecting copyright overseas, visit the Business Link website and the international section of the Intellectual Property Office (IPO).

 Intellectual Property protection overseas via Business Link site: bit.ly/bdyZZJ

 IPO Intellectual, property abroad: www.ipo.gov.uk/types/otherprotect/otherprotect-abroad.htm

Duties and taxes: Business Link guidance

"When a third country, i.e. a country outside the European Union (EU), receives your goods, it may charge duty. A third country may also charge an equivalent of VAT or purchase tax. Business Link explains the different types of taxes and how to use the UK Trade Tariff to find out what duties and taxes might have to be paid on goods when they are imported from outside the EU."

Source: Business Link bit.ly/9Cznsu

Insurance

Contact your insurance provider or broker to ensure you are protected for safe transit of your goods and for receipt of payment. Approach insurance providers for freight/shipping insurance (if not provided by your courier company), payment protection and professional indemnity if providing services.

- Direct Line: www.directline.co.uk
- Hiscox: www.hiscox.co.uk
- Simply Business: www.simplybusiness.co.uk

Certificates of origin

Your overseas client may request a certificate of origin. Apply for this online via the British Chambers of Commerce: **bit.ly/a7nQZH**

Distance selling regulations

If you sell goods or services to consumers via the internet, mail order or by phone, you are obliged to comply with the Consumer Protection (Distance Selling) Regulations 2000. The key features of the regulations are:

- You must offer consumers clear information including details of the goods or services offered, delivery arrangements and payment, the supplier's details and the consumer's cancellation right before they buy (known as prior information).

- This information should be provided in writing.

- The consumer has a period of seven working days from delivery of the items to cancel their contract with you.

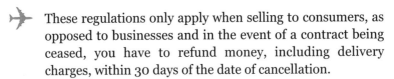

✈ These regulations only apply when selling to consumers, as opposed to businesses and in the event of a contract being ceased, you have to refund money, including delivery charges, within 30 days of the date of cancellation.

✈ Distance Selling Regulations: www.oft.gov.uk/about-the-oft/legal-powers/legal/distance-selling-regulations

Useful links

✈ Exporting basics via Business Link: bit.ly/bI8B23

✈ Institute of Export: www.export.org.uk

Admin checklist

Run through this checklist to ensure full compliance on reporting, safe transit of goods and peace of mind!

Action	Completed
I have completed the appropriate documentation and proof of export	✓
I have adequate insurance cover	✓
Sales from exports are reported on my tax return	✓
I comply with rules and regulations such as those for distance selling	✓
IP protection has been considered	✓
Any local regulations relating to matters such as product design and health & safety have been assessed	✓
There is agreement in place between me and my client as to who covers the cost of any duties or import taxes	✓

SUCCESS STORY

Ruby Pseudo

Jenny Owen adopted the pseudonym Ruby Pseudo as a writer and applied the same name to a business she started in March 2008. The business is a global youth planning and research consultant agency that works for top clients across the world.

Whilst employed at international PR agency Edelman, Ruby was involved in global trend research projects for brands including Nike and Unilever and this work continued when Ruby went solo. The business grew and Ruby didn't stay solo for long as work came in from companies wanting an insight into the youth market that Ruby could provide.

> "Our first big global project was a seminal moment for us; we were flying people to Tokyo and working with kids in Romania and Belgium for the first time, it was amazing, terrifying and a really big project for us all. There were three of us at the time, there are now ten and we do that kind of research everyday."

Ruby's clients mainly find her through the company blog or by word-of-mouth recommendation. Relations and conversations with clients are kept intact as Ruby and the team arrange face-to-face meetings when they are in the countries of clients and, in between times, send on links, news, and interviews they think will be of interest.

> "We also tend to write things on the blog that we believe will interest our clients. In that respect there are various 'invisible' ways to stay connected."

With the US now accounting for over 50% of her annual turnover, Ruby expects business from North America to keep on growing.

"Our network in America is really strong and we're blessed to work with some amazing kids out there from various backgrounds and lifestyles; members of the Crips in Los Angeles, Latin Kings from Spanish Harlem, film directors from Portland and sponsored skaters in Austin, for example. One of our team has also just spent 10 weeks in South America building the network there, so we're strengthening our contacts and gatekeepers all the time.

Without international contacts advising you, you're really just desk researching. We prefer genuine insights, straight from the kids, in their own words. It's how we always prefer to do business and is, I would argue, what we have built our reputation on."

Ruby is now investing time researching opportunities in Asia and Russia, both places where she sees a burgeoning youth culture and scene. This company is most certainly going places.

  www.rubypseudo.com

@ruby_pseudo

Customer service

Delivering good customer service is about getting your product or service to the customer on time and within budget. It's also about keeping in touch and maintaining strong lines of communication so that customers will want to continue buying what you have to offer. Here are the key elements of this and a number of tools and applications that can help you accomplish them.

Answering questions

Offer online customer support without having to be personally available 24/7. Instead, have your community help each other through Get Satisfaction, a tool that enables user-powered customer service.

> "It's a social support application for engaging your customer community to reduce support costs, build buzz and collect feedback."

It's a perfect tool for any business trading overseas and across time zones; you avoid leaving customers waiting for an answer as your community and customers help each other reach the answers. Your input is welcome, but at a time to suit you! Start with the basic product at $19 per month.

 www.getsatisfaction.com

@getsatisfaction

Avoid time zone tragedy

Avoid upsetting customers by calling them at 3am with a business query by turning to page 229 for a listing of time zones in major export territories.

Attend meetings and calls

Say 'hello' and talk business with co-workers and clients with these online tools and services:

- Dimdim – allows you to attend live meetings, demonstrations and webinars (**www.dimdim.com**, **@dimdim**).

- Pow Wow Now – free conference calling at 'Open Access' level. Priced packages also available (**www.powwownow.co.uk**, **@powwownow**).

- Skype – free and easy-to-use conference calls for Skype users (**www.skype.com**, **@skype**).

➤ Tinychat – group video conferencing for free
(www.tinychat.com, @tinychat).

➤ GoToWebinar – host a meeting of many and present to potential customers by inviting them to join you for an interactive webinar
(www.gotowebinar.com, @gotowebinar).

> "I have clients abroad and regularly cartoon for a site in the USA. I love the extra five hours I get on USA deadlines!"
>
> – *Colin Shelbourn, cartoonist and successful exporter*
>
> (www.shelbourn.com)

Manage projects

As your business expands overseas, so also will the network of international contacts with whom you are working – especially if yours is a service-based business. Keep in touch and keep on time and within budget for clients by making the most of project-management and collaboration tools that connect people across the globe:

➤ Basecamp – allows you to create projects, invite people to view them, upload files and make comments. It's effective online project management that can be accessed from anywhere (www.basecamphq.com).

➤ Google Docs – share documents via Google with Google Docs. You can edit on the move, choose who accesses documents and share changes in real-time (docs.google.com).

➤ Glasscubes – this tool offers project management, collaboration and CRM (customer-relationship management) all in one package (www.glasscubes.com, @glasscubes).

➤ Huddle – offers simple and secure online workspaces. Huddle is hosted so there's no software to download and it's free to get started (www.huddle.net, @huddle).

"Huddle makes it possible for people to connect and work with each other regardless of their location. Fuelled by the rapid rise in remote and online working, people across the globe use Huddle to share files, manage projects and workflows, control and distribute information, suggest and discuss ideas and hold online meetings, as well as connect with colleagues, customers, partners and suppliers. It makes it easy to work with other people inside and outside companies, across boundaries and time zones."

– *www.huddle.net*

✈ Crossloop.com – share pictures, collaborate on documents, offer training, or transfer and access files via this screen-sharing and collaborative tool site (**www.crossloop.com**, **@crossloop**).

✈ Show Document – share documents via this web collaboration platform. Upload files, mark them up and chat to discuss ideas and changes (**www.showdocument.com**, **@showdocument**).

✈ There are other technologies you can adopt to ensure your business travels with you, such as a webmail system that allows access to emails from anywhere, a remote desktop offering files and folders on the go, or web-based office system like Google Apps (**www.google.com/apps**) or Open Office (**www.openoffice.org**) so the entire business is stored online and in easy reach from anywhere.

"All international markets are different and require knowledge, although I have found the basic business principles are fairly universal. Most importantly – listen to your customers!"

– *David Sandy, Integreat Media*

"If you visit the US five or more times a year, get a pay-as-you-go US smart phone. The calls are cheaper and it pays for itself in hotel wi-fi savings."

– *Richard Moross, Moo.com*

SUCCESS STORY

Sarah Cooper, Cows From My Window

Sarah Cooper had always wanted to live overseas and do some form of work that did not tie her to a particular location. Having relished the energy of Beijing when she'd visited on a holiday, and ready for a move with baby daughter Elsa, the travelling twosome got on a plane and moved to China!

That was four years ago. After starting and growing a successful coaching business from her home in Beijing, Sarah has returned to the UK and resumed trade in Bristol. The company continues to be international in nature.

"I am a career coach and my clients tend to be mid-career professionals who are unfulfilled in traditional corporate careers. I have clients based in China, the Netherlands, the US and here in the UK. It's technology that makes this perfectly possible."

Sarah is a big fan of Skype, using the free Skype-to-Skype service to hold calls on a one-to-one basis, and a free conference service for group calls. She's a customer of International Boost with TalkTalk, which allows calls anywhere in the world (for under 60 minutes) for £2 per month, and working with two virtual PAs (in China and the US) Sarah keeps in close contact using Google Docs.

"You don't have to be a technical whizz to set these systems up. I manage to communicate with clients and secure new ones through Skype calls, a newsletter powered by Aweber and conference calling. The best thing is I don't need an in-house IT team to keep it ticking over!"

With ideas for new businesses in mind and low-cost technology tools at her disposal, Sarah is realising her dream of running a business that could be managed from practically anywhere.

www.cowsfrommywindow.com

@thecowscoach

Useful links

 Skype – www.skype.com

 International Boost with Talk Talk – broadband.talktalk.co.uk/products/broadband/ boosts/international

Google Docs – docs.google.com

 FreeConferenceCall.com – www.freeconferencecall.com

 A Weber – www.aweber.com

Step 5: Go Local

Trade is increasing and you want to emphasise just how serious you are about your clients, their country, and its customs and culture. There are a number of ways to do this, from having your site translated into the local language, through to having a local-rate call number and making regular visits. This final section will help you look local and show commitment.

Website localisation and geo-targeting

These are two technical-sounding terms but they will simply make your site more visible and attractive to customers in overseas markets.

 Website localisation is the process of adapting your site to suit a local culture and/or language.

Geo-targeting is directing pages or websites towards users in specific locations.

The benefits of having parts of your site localised and geo-targeted are improved positioning in local search results and increased sales as customers appreciate the effort you have made.

Here are steps you can take to achieve these results.

Domain names

When tailoring your site for a local market or country, you could choose to have sub domains from your main .com site or invest in a country code top-level domain (ccTLD) such as .fr for France or .ru for Russia. This will improve search engine optimisation.

Registering for some country codes does require having a presence or registered company in the country, but you can check this with most major domain registration companies.

 NetNames: www.netnames.com

✈ GoDaddy: www.godaddy.com

✈ 123 Reg: www.123-reg.com

✈ 1and1: www.1and1.co.uk

International domains increase online audience

The Internet Corporation for Assigned Names and Numbers (ICANN) has recently announced the availability of new domain names in languages using non-latin characters such as Arabic, Chinese and Russian. This widens your options when considering the purchase of local domain names.

Local hosting

When Google presents search results, sites that are hosted in the country of the user conducting the search tend to appear higher than sites hosted outside. So local hosting could be a consideration when you start doing considerable business in an overseas territory.

> 66 Search engines are looking at the host location (IP) of websites to try and deliver the most relevant results for the searcher. Ideally, you'd have the ability to host your unique TLDs (top level domains) in-country. So, if you're targeting Germany, you need a .de website and to host this within Germany. 99
>
> *– Mark Jackson, president and CEO of Vizion Interactive, 'International SEO Challenges and Tips'*

Ask your domain registrar about their local hosting service provision.

Having looked at the technical aspect of domains and hosting, the next (and most important) aspect to explore is the content on your site and promotional materials, and how to present both to potential customers.

Translation

> 66 Whether you're selling car-parts to Columbia, or sail-boats to Spain, proper website localisation means you have to think beyond language to the exact dialect of your target market. For example, in Spain the word for car is coche, but in many Latin American countries coche is a baby-stroller. In the UK, a baby-stroller is a pram or a buggy, and if you're from Canada, a buggy is likely to be something you put your groceries in. The point is, you need to be wary of differences between dialects – this requires local linguists with local knowledge. 99
>
> *– Christian Arno, founder, Lingo24.com*

When you consider 75% of the Earth's population don't speak English and over 50% of all web searches are in a language other than English, it might be an idea to put 'translation of website' quite high on the to-do list. Whether it's a few pages or the full site, you can translate your site with a free tool such as Google Translate (**translate.google.com**) or commission a website translation specialist such as Lingo24.com or Applied Language Solutions.

✈ Lingo24.com: **www.lingo24.com**

✈ Applied Language Solutions: **www.appliedlanguage.com**

✈ Applied Language Solutions also offer a free translation toolbar at:
    www.appliedlanguage.com/trans/free_quick.aspx

Outside of your website, consider having introductory emails translated, interpreters for conference calls, and local language versions of print promotion materials.

Fast Fact:

Sales will increase with a localised version of a website, with visitors four times more likely to buy in their native language. Site stickiness is also increased, with visitors staying twice as long.
Source: Gavin Wheeldon, Applied Language Solutions

Even in English-speaking countries it's worth hiring a local to work with you who is able to advise on marketing and promotion messages. This way you're sure to be getting all the right nuances and avoiding any cultural hot waters. Find copywriters via freelance websites such as Elance.com and Bitsythis.com.

66 We are in a privileged position speaking one of the world's major languages, and we benefit in many ways from others' eagerness to gravitate towards the English-speaking world. But it is a dangerous assumption to go from there to believing that English is the only language needed for communication in the global economy. 99

– Sir Trevor McDonald, 'Talking World Class: The impact of language skills on the UK economy' published by National Centre for Languages

On a fast connection to China

Exports from the UK to China grew 31% in 2008-09. Want a piece of the action? Read this information on having your site structured for the Chinese market:
www.metafocusglobal.com/chinese-websites.asp

Imagery

Having images on your site that resonate with an international audience will stand you in good stead to convert audience to customers.

Lee Torrens, micro stock expert, says:

> "I expect businesses need to be a certain size before geographical customisation becomes worthwhile, but that size is probably not as big as many people expect. In stock photography there's a lot of regional customisation done at the bigger agencies. They not only customise the choice of photos they use in their marketing, but they also customise the language of the website, the spelling (British, US and Australian English all have different spelling), currencies offered, and whether measurements are shown in metric or imperial. I think a business that is geographically specific could easily benefit from customising the stock imagery and other elements of their marketing."

Source tailored images for your site – and offline promotion materials – from international stock image sites:

 Photos.com: www.photos.com

iStockphoto: www.istockphoto.com

Getty Images: www.gettyimages.com

 Search for Creative Commons licensed images you can use commercially from Flickr at compfight.com

SUCCESS STORY

Ann-Maree Morrison, Labels4Kids Limited

After a career as an accountant and management consultant, Ann-Maree Morrison decided she wanted to do something that involved earning a living *and* having time to spend with the kids. Not only were her three children the motivating factor for the business, they were also the source of the business idea. As her boys regularly lost their belongings, Ann-Maree decided a company producing labels for everything – rather than just clothing – would do well.

"We started the business at the beginning of 2005, selling a wide range of labels; from vinyl to stick-in and sew-on labels. It was in 2008 that orders from overseas started to come in. I wanted to see if orders would increase by having a site translated into the local language, so we had a site translated into German, French and Swedish. At the time, we were getting two orders per month from Germany, for example – it's now eight orders per day. Having a site in the local language made the world of difference and I haven't spent a penny on direct marketing abroad as customers find us through search engine results."

The company ships small parcels from the UK and these go from the highly-rated local Post Office. Hiring an international courier service would not be effective, as the cost of shipping the item could be more than the value of the item itself. Payment is received via PayPal and RBS Worldpay.

With sales now coming in rapidly from Germany, France and Sweden, Ann-Maree has plans to expand into Spain, Italy and Portugal, and has purchased domain names for these countries. She is also hoping to sell countrywide franchises abroad to expand the business so that overseas orders can be dealt with locally.

Ann-Maree's family continues to play a part in the business. At the ages of 13, 11 and 8, the boys are regularly found helping Mum with packing parcels in the home extension that's been built to cater for orders coming in from an increasing number of countries.

 www.labels4kids.com

@labels4kids

Useful links

 PayPal: www.paypal.com

RBS Worldpay: www.rbsworldpay.com

The ten most used languages on the web

English

Chinese

Spanish

Japanese

French

Portuguese

German

Arabic

Russian

Korean

Local presence

Make it easy for clients to contact you by having a local phone number and postal address. There are three main ways to achieve this:

1. international virtual office

2. international virtual number

3. international virtual PA.

1. International virtual office

A virtual office will give you the look and feel of a local presence, without the associated costs. You can have an office address displayed on your business cards and website, and a receptionist to take calls, without having to buy an actual office and staff it up.

A virtual office means benefiting from:

✈ **A prime business address** – Choose an address that suits your company brand and image and one that is close to customers. This address can then be displayed on company promotion materials.

✈ **Mail handling** – Your virtual office provider will receive mail and parcels on your behalf and forward them to your preferred destination.

✈ **Call handling** – Have calls taken in local time zones and by a professional receptionist. Calls are taken in your company name and re-routed immediately to you or, if you're in meetings (or sleeping!), messages are passed on via email and text.

✈ **PA services** – Depending on the package you choose, a virtual office may also come with PA services; assistance with tasks such as typing, printing and booking travel.

The company with the widest global coverage is workplace-solutions provider Regus. With centres in 85 countries, 500 cities and 1,100 locations, you can be pretty sure that, no matter where you want to be, Regus will be able to accommodate you. When it comes to virtual offices, the company offers three packages: 'mailbox plus', 'telephone answering' and 'virtual office' (which is mailbox and telephone answering combined). The price of the package will depend on the services you choose, as well as the location, but start at £60 per month.

www.regus.co.uk/virtualoffices/products/default.htm#mailbox

66 We specialise in computer-related financial and accounting services and wanted to be closer to our international clients whilst retaining a professional image. The Regus virtual office provided us with a well-respected business address at a competitive price. Our base in Paris allows us to be highly mobile and project a world-class image. 99

– Myron Ratnavale, director, Geneva Consulting Group

See pages 144 and 163 for more details on how Regus can help your business go global.

Here are three sites offering links to local virtual office providers across all continents:

✈ eOffice:
    www.eoffice.net/locations/locations.html

✈ Instant Offices:
    www.instantoffices.com/Solutions/virtual-offices.aspx

✈ Easyoffices.com:
    www.easyoffices.com/virtual-offices

Top of the block

The most popular Regus virtual office locations worldwide are (drum roll, please):

1. New York, New York City – Chrysler Building
2. London, Berkeley Square
3. Sydney, Citigroup Centre
4. Illinois, Chicago – West Loop 200 South Wacker
5. Paris, Champs Elysées
6. Beijing, Kerry Centre
7. California, San Francisco – One Embarcadero
8. Tokyo, Otemachi 1st Square
9. Sao Paulo, Rochavera – Morumbi
10. Massachusetts, Boston – 60 State Street

2. International virtual number

Sign up to an international virtual number and not only do you get a local number to promote to clients, it also means they only pay a local rate when calling.

66 The advantage is that people overseas can call you for the price of a local call if you choose a virtual number in their area code. You can have as many lines as you like and maintain a local presence anywhere you choose. 99

– *Vonage.co.uk*

The key providers are:

Vonage – This company offers international dialling codes across 17 countries for a one-off activation fee of £5.99 and ongoing monthly subscription of £2.99 or £5.99 per month.

 www.vonage.co.uk/international-virtual-phone-numbers-uk

Skype – Buy a SkypeIn number in one of over 25 locations. As with Vonage, the online number uses the internet to route the call and so saves money for the person making the call. You can pick up the call at no cost to you wherever in the world you are logged into Skype. The cost is $18 for three months or $60 for a full year, with up to 50% off this cost with the purchase of a monthly subscription.

 www.skype.com/intl/en-us/features/allfeatures/online-number

Call me!

For international dialling codes visit

www.countrycallingcodes.com

3. International virtual PA

Another option is to hire a virtual PA or virtual assistant (VA) who operates from the country in which you wish to be represented and can take calls on your behalf, routing messages back to you, as well as completing other required tasks. The benefit of working with a VA is you get all the benefits of having a personal assistant without taking on the cost of a full time member of staff. Self-employed VAs are self-motivated so they get the job done on time and within budget. Identify a VA through freelance and industry websites:

✈ Elance: www.elance.com

✈ Bitsy: www.bitsythis.com

✈ oDesk.com: www.odesk.com

✈ International Virtual Assistants Association: www.ivaa.org

✈ International Association of Virtual Assistants: www.iava.org.uk

---

Get the Local Look: by post

Royal Mail has a product called 'Local Look' that allows you to send mail from the UK that looks like it originated in the country to where it is being sent.

"Supply us with details of where your campaign is being sent, the volume and size and we will let you know the options that exist to each country. The minimum volume requirement is 300 items per posting but it does vary by country so please check with our team of international consultants."

Source: Royal Mail International site: bit.ly/c8Mmkb

"Target one country at a time and really work out the cultural issues in depth. You'll win customers over to your way of working by doing this."

– Laura Bond

Visiting and business etiquette

Sales are coming in, relationships with customers and partners are getting ever stronger and you've decided it's time to visit the country. Take on board these travel tips for a successful mission.

Cultural and business etiquette

Spend time learning local phrases and something about the culture and customs of the country you're visiting.

66 Expressions and gestures that mean one thing in a given culture may mean something else in another. There can be differences in the way people greet each other and even how people are supposed to dress for a business meeting. There is no doubt taking the time and effort to learn, understand and show respect for your potential, or existing, client's culture and business etiquette will help secure and boost sales. 99

– Jessica Houghton, Expert Language Solutions, www.expertlanguages.com

See pages 170 to 222 for common business phrases in the UK's top 30 exported to nations. See pages 231 to 232 for an outline cultural briefing, and visit the UKTI website and Kwintessential for detailed notes on culture and business etiquette by country.

 UKTI: **www.ukti.gov.uk/export/countries.html**

 Kwintessential:
www.kwintessential.co.uk/resources/country-profiles.html

 Fast Fact:

Export businesses that are proactive in their use of language and cultural skills achieve on average 45% more sales.

Source: British Chambers of Commerce

Speaking your client's language

Jessica Houghton believes there are benefits to be had in speaking the same language as your client – and these advantages are both business and personal.

Everyone speaks English, right? Well, not exactly. According to the CIA World Fact Book, only 5.6% of the world's total population speaks English as a first language. That number doubles when people who speak English as a second or third language are counted. By conservative estimates, that implies that well over four-fifths of the world's population doesn't speak English. Here are the reasons to learn:

Better communication – English may be widely taught, but that doesn't mean it's *remembered*. In a recent EU Eurobarometer poll, barely a third of French people said they could speak English, despite having learnt it at school, and this pattern was similar across Europe. Even when others speak English, there's a definite advantage to being able to talk to them in their own language, even if it's just a few words. It shows you've made an effort and strengthens the relationship.

Useful when travelling – Learning the native language puts you at an advantage in that it allows you to travel off the beaten path and discover the authenticity, i.e. less touristy side, of the country. It helps in many situations; asking for directions, ordering food, and striking up conversation with the locals.

Sharpens the mind – When you learn a new language, you exercise the language faculties of your brain, boosting communication skills in general. In a way, language learning is a 'two-for-one' offer. You find a new way to express yourself in another tongue, while enhancing your abilities in your native language at the same time!

Jessica Houghton is founder of Expert Language Solutions (www.expertlanguages.com)

  66 If customers ask questions in their own language, write back to them in their own language (Google translate is like an extra employee!). 90% of these customers will typically buy, as they perceive you as having outstanding customer service. They want to be able to trust a foreign buyer, and this is a good way to demonstrate this. 99

– John Pemberton, Give Me Designer Clothing Global

  66 I'm in China for a month, overseeing production and making a start on our next season's collection. My Chinese is still rubbish. Thank goodness for modern technology; this would be impossible without it. Google translate is my new best friend! 99

– Janan Leo, CocoRose London

What to pack

The technology people at HP have come up with the ultimate office-in-a-backpack; a collection of items to make working whilst on the move an easy exercise. Those items are:

Core kit

There is some basic gear no mobile worker should be without:

✈ A small, light computer such as the HP Mini which is energy efficient and can last hours on a single charge.

✈ A smart phone means you can check email, view websites and even read and edit documents.

✈ Power management in Microsoft Windows can extend battery life (bit.ly/3yBRPa) but it's wise to take a charger. Taking an extra battery or choosing a long-life battery for your notebook can keep you going all day.

✈ To access the internet, you'll either need a wireless network or – to get connected from nearly anywhere – a mobile broadband connection. Some notebooks have a slot for a SIM card so you can connect to mobile broadband without any extra equipment. Alternatively, you can buy a plug-in 3G modem.

Handy accessories

Carefully chosen accessories will add minimal weight to your bag and can make you more productive:

- Noise-cancelling headphones. Loud cafe? Busy train? A good pair of headphones can give you peace and quiet. And if you take lots of phone calls, consider a Bluetooth headset too.

- A mouse and wrist rest. Working on a laptop can be an ergonomic nightmare. Carry a portable mouse and – depending on your laptop – a wrist rest to stave off aches and pains.

- Mobile working can pose some security risks, too. To stop people seeing what you're working on in public, consider using a screen guard to block their view. And to avoid drawing attention to your kit when you're in the street, don't use an obvious laptop bag. Instead, use a padded laptop sleeve inside a nondescript bag.

  It's not all about electronics. Stick a decent notepad and a few pens into your bag too!

Matthew Stibbe of Articulate Marketing wrote this post for the HP Business Answers blog (bit.ly/aKgfEa)

I hear you!

Download a free talking phrasebook in a range of six European languages. Available for the iPhone and Nokia handsets or as a podcast via iTunes.

www.coolgorilla.mobi

A warm welcome

Before travelling, check out world weather conditions at
www.metoffice.gov.uk/weather

66 Brazilian consumers still have a great thirst for brands that pay attention to them. If you want to make a difference, come prepared to truly know your public and interact with them. And very important, don't forget the sunscreen! 99

– Interview with Anna Valenzuela, Brazilian entrepreneur and co-founder of Migux, Brazil's largest online network for children. Source: The Next Women (bit.ly/99tdIN).

Where to work

With cultural etiquette in hand, a few local words in your head and a tech pack on your back, the question is where to work in the host country. What locations offer both a professional image and a comfortable place to do business? Hotel lobbies are certainly an option, as are Regus business centres.

As outlined on page 135, Regus is the world's largest provider of workspace solutions. Being a Regus Businessworld card-carrying member entitles you to a touchdown facility in whichever city or country you're doing business. Access the offices to work quietly, arrange to meet clients in the business lounges and cafés, and benefit from the virtual office after you've headed home. Offices and space can be hired by the hour or day.

 Regus Businessworld membership card options:
www.regus.co.uk/businessworld/cards.html

"Working internationally, or exporting, can increase turnover, keep you motivated and generally improve overall business performance. Whatever the reason you are looking to work internationally, it should be stimulating, inspiring and fun."

– Christine Losecat, China UK Partners

A memorable exchange

Richard Moross is founder of Moo.com, a company that has been printing stylish business cards, mini cards and more since 2004. With 70% of Moo's business being outside the UK, Richard travels a lot. And whilst on the move, he takes photos of places visited and meals eaten. These images end up on his business cards, which act as the ice breaker in meetings as he tells the story behind the pictures. He says:

"The point of having a business card is to:

 make a connection

 create a relationship

leave something with the recipient that reminds them of you.

Have cards you can place on the table that tell a story. Use that card as a sales tool, for sure, but also show cultural appreciation in global markets by maybe having localised versions relating to that country and/or customer."

www.moo.com

Calculating the cost

Work out how much your travels will set you back with the xe.com travel-expenses calculator:
www.xe.com/tec/table.shtml

Useful travel site links

Rough Guide – **www.roughguides.com**
Fodors – **www.fodors.com**
Lonely Planet – **www.lonelyplanet.com/uk**
Wiki Travel – **www.wikitravel.org**

Jettisoning jet lag

"Eat when the locals eat, sleep when the locals sleep, drink lots of water, and stick to your regular consumption of caffeine."

– Alex Hornbake, oDesk blog team

SUCCESS STORY

Amanda Ruiz, Humm Peruvian Knitwear

Little did Amanda Ruiz know that marrying her Peruvian husband, Manuel, would lead to her starting a business selling ethically produced Peruvian handmade knitwear to customers from many countries.

> "When Manuel and I had our first child in 2005, we were given lots of beautiful and bright gifts from relatives in Peru; ponchos, chullos (earflap hats) and cardigans. These were so widely admired that I thought, why not share this discovery with other mums and indeed everyone in the UK? It was clear there was a gap in the market for clothing that was different to the offerings of the high street, so we launched the business in September 2007."

The company and the couple combined a family visit to Peru with finding suppliers, looking into the logistics of exporting and meeting local artisans. Amanda wanted to be sure the products were ethically produced, so visited the factory to see the working conditions.

> "I personally confirmed all this, as I speak fluent Spanish and chatted with lots of artisans."

The knitted products are made in Peru but, with an online store, they are sold all over the world. What Amanda has discovered is that the gap in the market she identified was not just in the UK. Regular enquiries and orders come from Turkey, Hungary, Australia, Cyprus, the USA, Norway, Sweden, France, Austria and Germany. Orders and enquiries are received on the back of the company being found in search engine results and through word of mouth recommendation.

"We are also building up a following on our Peruvian Knitwear Facebook fan page. It's a very international following with fans from the USA, Peru, Greece, Spain, Norway…and counting!"

The company accepts international payment by PayPal and Amanda ensures she receives payment before shipping products and that the shipment is fully trackable.

The plan is to increase international sales over the next 12 months through a design collaboration with Brandon Mably of the Kaffe Fasset studio, who travels across the world teaching the art of combining colours for textiles. Translation of the website is also on the to-do list, with the first countries to have localised pages being in Scandinavia.

"Within the next year, I think our best-selling countries will be the USA, France and Australia. One of my drivers in setting up the business was to provide work for Peruvian artisans and I'm delighted that, in selling to customers overseas, their craftsmanship will be seen all over the world."

 www.hummshop.com

@peruvianknitwr

Deepening cultural relations

As mentioned throughout the book, doing business overseas is not all about business; it also leads to deepening cultural understanding and relations.

This was part of the motivation when the British Council launched TN2020 to develop the special relationship that exists between the UK and the US.

66 The network encourages members to collaborate on global issues, one of which is trade, and even though this is not a trading network in itself, an Italian and American met at the gatherings and have since started an olive oil business together! Business connections can be made when introducing people to each other but when you bring together people from different countries, backgrounds and viewpoints, that's when it gets really interesting. Together, these people can solve anything! 99

– Jacqui Allan, Assistant Director USA, British Council in Washington and Head of TN2020 www.britishcouncil.org/tn2020.htm

Network member, Rajeeb Dey agrees:

66 Forming business links internationally can deepen cultural relations and being part of a network such as the British Council's TN2020 is a springboard to developing these contacts and partnerships abroad. It brings together a diverse network of emerging leaders from North America and Europe; from the world of business, arts, civil society, media, the public sector and beyond, who all share similar ideals of improving society. As a relatively new member of the network I hope to learn more about the countries represented and the scope to doing business in those regions. 99

PART III:

Where to Go for Help

Government support

There are a number of public bodies and private sector companies on hand to advise and guide you in the process of going global.

UK Trade & Investment

66 We have one of the best trade support networks in the world, with expert staff from across the globe and across a range of sectors who are ideally placed to help you realise your potential. 99

– Andrew Cahn, chief executive, UKTI

With a staff of 2,500 people, of which over 1,000 are located overseas in 96 markets, the government's UK Trade & Investment (UKTI) is well placed to assist small companies in taking their business to the world.

The agency has two parent departments in the form of the Department for Business, Innovation and Skills (BIS), and the Foreign and Commonwealth Office (FCO). In the 12 months to March 2010, UKTI assisted 23,700 companies in exploiting opportunities in overseas markets. Key programmes on offer are outlined in the box on page 152.

Passport to export

International trade advisors review a company's readiness for international business through capability assessments. Support is on offer to visit potential markets as well as help with action plans, training and ongoing support.

Overseas market introduction service

Delivered online, this provides direct contact with staff in overseas embassies and consulates, offering tailored market research, help in finding agents and distributors, and access to embassy facilities when visiting a particular country.

Export communications review

Provides help with the linguistic and cultural aspects of doing business overseas and offers companies a variety of options and advice, including cultural awareness reviews and communication planning. Delivered by the British Chambers of Commerce (BCC).

Export marketing research scheme

Aimed at exporters wanting to carry out detailed research when considering entry into new overseas markets. It provides free expert marketing research advice and, for eligible small and medium-sized companies, a grant of up to 50% of the agreed cost of market research projects.

Market visit support

MVS assists groups of UK companies in attending overseas trade shows and taking part in group market visits/trade missions.

Tradeshow access programme (TAP)

Grant support for eligible companies, new and less experienced exporters, to exhibit overseas.

Online business opportunities

Over 400 opportunities per month are made available to UK businesses registered for alerts via the website. Register at www.ukti.gov.uk.

The first point of contact you will have with UKTI is an international trade advisor (ITA). Locate your closest ITA by typing in your postcode on the export home page (www.ukti.gov.uk/export.html) or visit the Regional UKTI contacts page (www.ukti.gov.uk/export/unitedkingdom/contactus.html).

Subscribe to UKTI's free quarterly publication 'Springboard' (springboard.managemyaccount.co.uk).

Scottish Development International (SDI)

This agency helps Scotland-based companies develop their international trade. It offers a range of services to assist such businesses entering foreign markets for the first time or expanding overseas operations.

> " Successful international trade requires planning, knowledge and skills, plus a support network and contacts. We aim to provide flexible support designed to meet your specific needs in the international marketplace. "
>
> *– SDI*

Support is offered across a number of areas:

- gaining an overview of international business
- developing your international strategy
- understanding new international markets
- developing skills for international business
- exploring new markets
- setting up operations in new markets
- international business opportunities.

You need to research each programme, as some are only open to companies with annual turnover in excess of £400,000. Schemes open to all small businesses include:

Overseas market introduction service

Research reports are delivered by UK Trade and Investment (UKTI) commercial officers based in posts overseas. There is a cost, with reports starting at £490 (bit.ly/d6ndF8).

Enterprise Europe Scotland

Open to all small businesses in Scotland, this offers a free service of market information and specialist advice on the European Union, including events on doing business in European markets (www.enterprise-europe-scotland.com/sct).

British Airways flight discount offer

Take advantage of a 15% discount on BA flights from the UK. Bookings need to be made by February 2011 and travel completed by February 2012 (bit.ly/9t17ZP).

Useful links

✈ Scottish Development International trade services: www.sdi.co.uk/export

✈ GlobalScot – An online business network of Scottish expats around the world (www.globalscot.com)

Invest Northern Ireland (INI)

Invest Northern Ireland is the economic development agency for Northern Ireland. The agency works to strengthen the Northern Irish economy and part of its remit is to increase export levels. This happens through five main categories of export support.

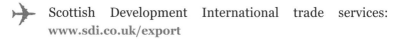

66 Our cluster of programmes and services will support you throughout the export process: from building your export skills and knowledge, to helping with researching markets through to assisting you once you have decided on a target market. 99

– INI

Export skills and knowledge workshops

Workshops are open to all export-focused companies in any sector. It is not necessary to be an Invest NI client business to participate but workshop registration is required.

www.investni.com/index/grow/export/exportworkshops.htm

Market entry support

Utilise a network of trade and marketing mentors, and advisors through the export advisory service. You can get help carrying out market assessments, identifying the best approach for market entry, and exploring market entry strategies focusing on agents and distributors.

www.investni.com/index/grow/export/market_entry_support. htm

In-market support

Access local knowledge and contacts through the trade advisory service or benefit from introductions to potential partners via the strategic business alliance service. Practical support is also on offer through the provision of serviced workspace and meeting facilities in a number of Invest NI overseas offices and business-incubation services for companies looking to do business in the Middle East.

www.investni.com/index/grow/export/in-market_support.htm

Market visits

Make the most of participation in trade missions and exhibitions to test the market, gather intelligence, attract suppliers, appoint agents and make sales.

www.investni.com/index/grow/export.htm

Business information centre and Enterprise Europe Network

Benefit from Northern Ireland's most comprehensive range of directories, company databases and business intelligence to research markets and identify new customers.

bit.ly/d9RqpC

www.enterpriseeuropeni.com

Useful links

✈ Invest NI help for exporters:
www.investni.com/index/grow/export.htm

✈ Guidance for exporters:
www.nibusinessinfo.co.uk/internationaltrade

International Business Wales (IBW)

The international trade arm of the Welsh Assembly, this agency is tasked with helping Welsh businesses trade with the rest of the world.

❝ The Welsh Assembly government is 100% behind ambitious businesses ready to enter or expand their global markets. We can do two things for you; the groundwork to help make your business ready for international trade, and finding you the deals and partnerships to make things happen. ❞

– IBW

International Business Wales offers:

✈ professional guidance to develop export potential and gain deeper knowledge of international trading

✈ assistance to develop trading relationships, including a comprehensive international-events programme.

One of the support services is the ITO (international trade opportunities) programme. This scheme offers access to a network of market and sector specialists in a number of key markets identified by the Welsh Assembly Government. Specialists offer local knowledge, connections, advice and on the ground support. There is a cost involved but for eligible companies there is support available to subsidise the fees.

Register your interest for the ITO programme at: bit.ly/cE107H

Potential exporters are requested to contact International Business Wales so that specific and tailored support can be provided.

Useful links

✈ International trade support:
www.ibwales.com/international-trade

✈ Calendar of overseas trade events:
www.ibwales.com/international-trade/international-trade-events

✈ Newsletter registration:
www.ibwales.com/news/newsletters

Other

British Chambers of Commerce

The British Chambers of Commerce (BCC) is the national body for a network of accredited Chambers of Commerce across the UK. Each local Chamber provides services to the businesses, including advice on international trade development.

Chambers deliver a number of UK Trade & Investment programmes, offer export training, and can assist with any questions about documentation.

The chambers' 'Export Zone' newsletter is produced three times a year. Register or read back issues at
www.britishchambers.org.uk/zones/export/export-zone-newsletter.html

Visit the BCC Export Zone for country guides and exporting tips: www.britishchambers.org.uk/zones/export

 British Chamber guide to global markets: www.exportguides.co.uk/global

Private sector providers

This book and the *Go Global* project would not have been possible without support from some private sector partners, all of whom offer valuable services and products to UK companies trading with the world. Here is how they can help you too!

Alibaba.com

Alibaba.com is a global trade marketplace, enabling you to source suppliers and connect with customers anywhere in the world.

Founded in 1999 by Jack Ma, a former English teacher from Hangzhou, Alibaba.com was started as a trading platform for small manufacturers to sell their wares. The site has grown to become the premier online marketplace for small companies around the world, where they can identify trading partners, interact with each other and conduct business online.

Together the Alibaba Group of companies form a community of more than 47 million registered users from over 240 countries and regions.

The site has just under 700,000 registered users in the UK, accounting for 6% of all registered users on Alibaba.com's international marketplace, and growing at a rate of 22,000 new members each month.

On the Alibaba website you can research your market by reading the country and industry reports, and then build business by buying and selling with trusted partners.

66 AliExpress, a new wholesale marketplace, has been designed to help the smallest businesses become more competitive by allowing business owners to tailor orders from international suppliers to their specific needs. Users can search for and source a huge variety of products online at the most competitive prices, place smaller-quantity orders and make instant online transactions through PayPal – all with the added protection and peace of mind of an escrow service to protect buyers and sellers. 99

– Alibaba.com

Maggie Choo is Alibaba's Director for Europe, the Middle East and Africa:

"The internet has opened up a host of opportunities for businesses, however small, to reach out, connect and trade easily and securely online.

And Alibaba.com has made the process simple and efficient for anyone to try their hand at international trading. It costs nothing to set up an account and get started. Many users find this is the first step on a journey that delivers significant extra revenue. We already have some 700,000 UK companies trading across the platform and we are dedicated to helping these and other organisations trade more profitably.

Showing the nation's market traders just how quickly and easily they can source goods online from domestic and foreign suppliers is just one of the ways we can achieve this."

To find out more about Alibaba vist:

✈ Alibaba.com (**www.alibaba.com**)

✈ Alibaba country profiles: **bit.ly/b85dNM**

✈ Alibaba industry reports: **bit.ly/asA7aQ**

HP

HP is one of the world's largest technology companies. The company is headquartered in California and from here, and a global network of offices, it serves over one billion customers, in more than 170 countries.

The company ships over 1 million printers per week and 48 million PC units each year. This is a global business that can help you do global business!

As well as their range of notebooks for working on the go, you can pose your technical questions to the company via HP Business Answers, or the Tech Tuesday Twitter #watercoolermoment, sponsored by HP for community sourced answers.

The company can answer questions on how to extend the life of your battery laptop, through to providing guidance on what machine is best for you and your business.

Providing you with technology tools and tips, HP is a safe partner to have around when doing business around the globe (and HP notebook power supplies are designed to work with US and UK voltages, which is a bonus!).

 www.hp.com/uk/goglobal

HP Business Answers:
bit.ly/cZhPgZ

PayPal

PayPal offers a safe and simple way to send and receive money online.

Regarded as the leading international payment platform, PayPal has more than 84 million active registered accounts (nearly 220 million total accounts) and is available in 190 markets. PayPal supports payments in 24 currencies and has localised websites in 20 markets, including Australia, Canada, China, France, Germany, the UK and the United States.

For online store owners, PayPal is easy to introduce and offers customers peace of mind that payment will be secure. The company offers three main products:

- ✈ website payments standard
- ✈ website payments pro
- ✈ express checkout.

When receiving payment through PayPal, you receive an email notification and money is credited to your PayPal account. You can then use your PayPal balance to make payments, or withdraw funds to your bank account. Say PayPal:

> "Because customers prefer using it, they will pay more through PayPal than through other payment methods. PayPal makes it easy for customers because they don't need to re-enter card details every time they buy."

There are no set-up charges, monthly fees or cancellation charges and fee levels vary depending on the volume of your sales.

How PayPal can help

For companies trading overseas, PayPal can help with:

- ✈ Offering a payment solution on your own site that customers will regard as safe and reliable. A payment option that accepts credit cards and payment in multiple currencies without any technical knowledge required on your part.

- ✈ Offering mobile payments as an option for customers on the move.

- ✈ Introductions to e-commerce partners that offer shopping carts and website builders.

Make contact

To find out more about PayPal, visit:

✈ PayPal products for business: bit.ly/alEuqb

✈ PayPal on twitter @PayPalUK

✈ In video: PayPal's 10 steps to e-commerce success (www.enterprisenation.com/content/AudioVideo.aspx)

✈ Via email: learnmore@paypal.com

Powa.com

Powa is the small business division of Venda.com, a supplier of safe and solid e-commerce sites powering brands such as Jimmy Choo, Tesco and Monsoon.

The small business owner who is going global can use their services to create an online store and be ready for customers from across the world when they come shopping. Building a store on Powa.com does not involve technical know-how and you can find a design expert from Powa's network to help fashion the site with your own branding and look and feel.

Within minutes, be up and running with a site that can take sales. Pick a pre-designed theme from a range of colour palettes and layouts. Customise the store with built-in tools to create a design that matches your brand and vision, and automatically create a page for every product in your inventory. No programming experience is required!

Powa sites come with search-engine optimisation built in. Your pages are coded with titles and descriptions based on page content, which helps search engines match your products to relevant searches. Each page also has a customisable and static URL (such as www.companyx.com/pinkpots.html) based on product search keywords, to help improve search rankings.

Dan Wagner, founder of Powa.com says:

> "Having created Venda as a powerful e-commerce platform for large retailers, I wanted small businesses to benefit from the same technology and reach. Powa.com was the result. We offer the sturdiness of a large e-commerce system at a price that small businesses can afford. We are seeing Powa customers leverage their online presence to sell into new countries and markets and we will continue to innovate and develop the Powa platform so it provides small and global businesses with all the tools they need."

Read on page 75 how Powa is helping a number of businesses on the Isle of Man sell from the island. To find out more about Powa as your online launch pad to the world, visit **www.powa.com**.

Regus

Regus is the world's leading global provider of innovative workspace solutions, with products and services ranging from fully equipped offices to professional meeting rooms, business lounges and the world's largest network of video communication studios. Regus delivers a new way to work, whether it's from home, on the road or from an office.

Over 800,000 clients a day benefit from Regus facilities spread across a global footprint of 1,100 locations in 500 cities and 85 countries, which allow individuals and companies to work wherever, however and whenever they want.

The company helps many small business to 'go global' with offerings such as Virtual Offices and Virtual PAs, incorporating a dedicated business address and mail and call handling services, use of office space and meeting rooms and the Businessworld scheme which entitles card holders to 'touchdown' in Regus business lounges across the globe.

Regus meeting, training and conference rooms are located at premier addresses in city centres, central business hubs and business parks with convenient access to major airports or public transport. Using the latest technology you can now locate your closest business centre and book space with the Regus app for the iPhone.

To find out more visit www.regus.co.uk

To download the Regus App for the iPhone visit reg.us/iphone-app

Shipwire.com

If you are considering local shipping as an option, where products are locally stored, picked and packed, Shipwire.com would like to be at the top of your consideration list.

Shipwire handles storage, packing, shipping and other logistical details from warehouses in the US, Canada and Europe, with more facilities scheduled to come online around the world.

Within a few clicks on Shipwire's site, you can arrange to have inventory sent to Shipwire warehouses, integrate Shipwire with your own site and start fulfilling customer orders in real-time.

Shipwire enables home-based start-ups, online entrepreneurs, seasonal businesses and exporters to have multiple warehouses and automated order fulfilment within easy reach. Rather than deal with the hassles of storage and shipping, leverage Shipwire so you spend time growing your business.

Plans start at $30 a month and are easy enough to operate online, with a setup process that takes less than 15 minutes. The company offers a free trial so you can try before you buy.

Headquartered in Palo Alto, California, Shipwire is led by a team that includes veterans from the software and logistics industries. Find out more at the following links:

- ✈ Free Shipwire software for do-it-yourself shipping: www.shipwire.com/anywhere
- ✈ Shipwire: www.shipwire.com
- ✈ Shipwire blog: www.shipwire.com/help/c/welcome/blog
- ✈ How local shipping can work for your business: www.shipwire.com/howitworks

Conclusion

I hope you have enjoyed this book and that it has shown just how possible it is to take your business to the world. It confirms you don't have to be a big business with a burly budget. What's required is a serious focus on your niche. With this focus you can achieve global reach through leveraging technology, delivering a great service, and promoting your success.

Concentrate on the aspects of business you do best and outsource the rest. Embrace social media. Trade online and strengthen links with customers through visiting them and learning about local customs and culture ... and maybe a little of the language!

What a privileged position we are in when our business acts as our passport. It is the passport to visit new places and meet interesting people. It is a passport to increased revenues, with the world really being our marketplace. Enjoy the experience of international trade and use this book as your guide.

Which only leaves me to say, as they say in English, French and Japanese:

Good Luck, Bonne Chance, Gambette Kudasai.

Emma Jones

emma@enterprisenation.com

twitter.com/emmaljones

Appendices

Appendix 1: Country profiles for the UK's top 30 export nations

The UK's top 30 export nations by value are:

1. USA
2. Germany
3. Netherlands
4. France
5. Ireland
6. Belgium-Luxembourg
7. Spain
8. Italy
9. China
10. Sweden
11. Switzerland
12. Hong Kong
13. UAE including Dubai
14. Japan
15. Canada
16. Singapore
17. Australia
18. India
19. Norway
20. Poland
21. Denmark
22. Russia
23. Saudi Arabia
24. Turkey
25. South Africa
26. South Korea
27. Brazil
28. Greece
29. Portugal
30. Czech Republic

Australia

Prime Minister: Julia Gillard

Population: 21.75 million

Level of trade with UK: "The UK sells more to Australia than to India or China and in 2008-09, two-way merchandise trade between Australia and the United Kingdom was worth approximately A$20.5 billion [£11.7 billion]."
Foreign & Commonwealth Office

Percentage of population with internet: 80.1%

Size of e-commerce market: 17 million with internet access, 80% of whom intended to make online purchases in the second half of 2010.

Local domain suffix: .AU

Currency: Australian Dollar

Time zone(s): Eastern, GMT+10; Central, GMT+9.30; Western, GMT+8

Traditional dish: Pavlova. Created to honour Russian dancer Anna Pavlova on a 1920s tour of the country (a claim pressed equally by New Zealand), this meringue-based pudding, topped with fruits and cream, is traditionally eaten at Christmas time.

Search engines: www.bing.com/?cc=au, www.google.com.au, au.yahoo.com
Local news feed (in English): www.theaustralian.com.au, www.abc.net.au/news

Belgium

Prime Minister: Yves Leterme

Population: 10.2 million

Level of trade with UK: "The UK is Belgium's fourth largest supplier and is the sixth largest market for UK exports. In 2004, Belgian exports to the UK amounted to €17.1bn, while Belgium's imports from the UK amounted to almost €15bn."
Foreign & Commonwealth Office

Percentage of population with internet: 77.8%

Size of e-commerce market: 8.1 million with internet access, 68% of whom intended to make online purchases in the second half of 2010.

Local domain suffix: .BE

Currency: Euro (€)

Time zone(s): Central European Time (CET), GMT+1

Traditional dish: *Mosselen-friet* (Dutch) or *moules-frites* (French): mussels and chips. Belgian chips are typically thicker than other nations' by several millimetres, and fried exclusively in animal fat; they claim to have invented them first, though France disputes this.

A few key phrases (from www.kwintessential.co.uk):

English	Flemish
Hello	Goeiendag/Hallo
Good morning	Goedemorgen
Good evening	Goedenavond
Good night	Goedenacht
Goodbye	Dag or Tot ziens
Yes	Ja
No	Nee
Please	Alstublieft
Thank you	Dank U
You're welcome	Zonder dank
Excuse me	Pardon
Sorry	Sorry
How are you?	Hoe gaat het met U/jou?
I'm fine thanks	Goed, bedankt
What's your name?	Hoe heet U'je?
My name is	Ik heet
Where are you from?	Vanwaar zijt U/ben je?
Do you speak English?	Spreekt U/spreek je Engels?
I don't understand	Ik begrijp het neit

See also: France.

Search engines: www.bing.com/?cc=be, www.google.be
Local news feed (in English): www.deredactie.be

Brazil

President: Luiz Inacio Lula da Silva (at time of writing – imminent change expected)

Population: 189.6 million

Level of trade with UK: "Brazil is the UK's most important trading partner in Latin America. [The UK's] market share is around 2%, with bilateral trade worth over £3bn in 2007, UK exports of £1.08bn and imports of £2.06bn."
Foreign & Commonwealth Office

Percentage of population with internet: 37.8%

Size of e-commerce market: 75.9 million with internet access, 84% of whom intended to make online purchases in the second half of 2010.

Local domain suffix: .BR

Currency: Real

Time zone(s): Brazil Eastern Time, GMT-3. There are three other time zones in Brazil, but Brazil Eastern Time covers the key trade areas of the country, including Rio, Sao Paulo and Brasilia.

Traditional dish: *Feijoada* stew. A mix of beans, beef and pork, often served with sausages and rice. Reputed to derive from ancient recipes arising out of what is now modern-day Portugal.

A few key phrases (from www.kwintessential.co.uk):

English	Portuguese
Hello	Bom dia
Good morning	Bom dia
Good evening	Boa tarde
Goodbye	Adeus
Yes/No	Sim/Não
Maybe	Talvez
Please	Se faz favour/Por favor
Thank you	Obrigado/a
You're welcome	De nada
Excuse me	Desculpe
Beautiful	belo
Better	melhor
Excellent	excelente
Good	bom/boa
Happy	feliz
Ill	doente
One more/another	mais um(a)

Search engines: www.bing.com/?cc=br, www.google.com.br, br.yahoo.com

Local news feed (in English): www.buenosairesherald.com, www.riotimesonline.com

Canada

Prime Minister: Stephen Harper

Population: 33.4 million

Level of trade with UK: "The value of UK goods exported to Canada totalled approximately £3.6 billion in 2008."
Foreign & Commonwealth Office

Percentage of population with internet: 77%

Size of e-commerce market: 26.2 million with internet access, 66% of whom intended to make online purchases in the second half of 2010.

Local domain suffix: .CA

Currency: Canadian Dollar

Time zone(s): Atlantic (GMT-4), Eastern (GMT-5), Central (GMT-6), Mountain (GMT-7), Newfoundland (GMT-3.30) and Pacific (GMT-8).

Traditional dish: Poutine, if you're in Quebec – fried potatoes, beef gravy and cheese curds. Its name derives from the English word 'pudding'. A Canadian pudding, however, is generally anything with maple syrup on it. The average UK price for this imported natural sweetener makes it more expensive per ml than petrol and wine.

Search engines: www.bing.com/?cc=ca, www.google.ca, www.yahoo.ca

Local news feed (in English): www.nationalpost.com, www.theglobeandmail.com

China

President: Hu Jintao

Population: 1.29 billion

Level of trade with UK: "China has been the UK's fastest growing export market since 2002 and in December 2007 became the largest export market in Asia for British goods. In 2007, the UK exported £3.781 billion of goods to China, an increase of 16% over the 2006 figures, and imported £18.795 billion, an increase of 23%. The UK is the EU's fourth largest exporter of goods to China, behind Germany, France and Italy."
Foreign & Commonwealth Office

Percentage of population with internet: 51.7%

Size of e-commerce market: 420 million with internet access, 95% of whom intended to make online purchases in the second half of 2010.

Local domain suffix: .CN

Currency: Yuan or Renminbi (RMB)

Time zone(s): China Standard Time, GMT+8

Traditional dish: Bird's nest soup (*jin wo*), a light brown soup made principally of the nests of swift birds found in southeast Asia. These nests are made of solidified saliva and dissolve in water to provide a popular and expensive meal that reputedly assists the libido, enhances the voice and alleviates asthma. A kilogram of white nests costs up to £1,200.

A few key phrases (from www.languagetutoring.co.uk
and www.kwintessential.co.uk).

English	Mandarin [Pinyin]
Hello	Ni hao
Goodbye	Zaijian
May I ask your name?	Nin guxing
My name is...	Wo xing
I am from	Wo shi cong...laide
Could you speak more slowly please?	Qing ni shuo man yidian hao ma?
I do not understand	Wo tingbudong
Telephone	dianhua
International call	guoji dianhua
Computer	diannao
Email	dianziyoujian, or just email
Internet	yinte wang/hulian wang
Where can I get online?	Wo zai nar keyi shang wang?
Are there any messages for me?	you meiyou liu hua?

English	Cantonese [Pinyin]
Hello, how are you?	nehih ho ma?
Fine	geih ho
Goodbye	baahih baahih/joih gin
Thanks	M goih
Excuse me	M goih
Do you speak English?	Nehih sik m sik gong ying man a?
I don't understand	Ngoh m mihng

Search engines: www.baidu.com, www.bing.com/?cc=cn,
www.google.cn, cn.yahoo.com
Local news feed (in English): www.globaltimes.cn

Czech Republic

Prime Minister: Jan Fischer

Population: 10.3 million

Level of trade with UK: "In 2008, UK exports to the Czech Republic were £1.5 billion. Czech exports to the UK were £3.5 billion in 2008."
Foreign & Commonwealth Office

Percentage of population with internet: 65.5%

Size of e-commerce market: 6.6 million with internet access, 83% of whom intended to make online purchases in the second half of 2010.

Local domain suffix: .CZ

Currency: Czech Crown

Time zone(s): Central European Time (CET), GMT+1

Traditional dish: Roast pork, dumplings and sauerkraut. The dumplings, curiously, tend to be served sliced, and can be mistaken for pork medallions or bread slices. Washed down with beer, and 'beer cheese' – a fearsomely strong soft cheese mixed with raw onions and mustard, enough to make your eyes water (as well as those of anyone you may happen to subsequently breathe near).

A few key phrases (from www.prague.tv):

English	Czech
Hello (formal)	Dobry den
Hello (informal)	Ahoj!
Goodbye	Na shledanou
Good evening	Dobry vecer
Good night	Dobrou noc
Yes (formal)	Ano
Yes (informal)	Jo or No
No	Ne
Excuse me	S dvolením
Sorry!	Prominte!
Please/You're welcome	Prosím
I understand	Rozumím
I don't understand	Nerozumím
How much is it?	Kolík to stoji?
Can you help me?	Muzete mi pomoci?

Search engines: www.google.cz
Local news feed (in English): www.ceskenoviny.cz/news,
www.praguepost.com

Denmark

Prime Minister: Anders Fogh Rasmussen

Population: 5.4 million

Level of trade with UK: "The Danes have a slight trade surplus with the UK but trade in either direction is about £4 billion annually." *Foreign & Commonwealth Office*

Percentage of population with internet: 86.1%

Size of e-commerce market: 4.7 million with internet access, 81% of whom intended to make online purchases in the second half of 2010.

Local domain suffix: .DK

Currency: Danish Krone

Time zone(s): Central European Time (CET), GMT+1

Traditional dish: Smoked eel in an open sandwich (or smørrebrød). More famous, of course, for bacon – a specialised export industry that was developed specifically for the lucrative UK market in the 1800s. By the 20th century, 90% of their exported swine were heading to Britain. In modern Denmark, whilst bacon exporting still flourishes, 75% of bacon sold and consumed domestically is imported.

A few key phrases (from **www.kwintessential.co.uk**):

English	Danish
Hello	Goddag/Hej (pol/inf)
Goodbye	Farvel
Yes	Ja
No	Nej
Thank you	Tak
Excuse me	Undskyld
May I/Do you mind?	Ma jeg/Tillader De?
What's your name?	Hvad hedder du?
My name is ...	Jeg hedder ...
Where are you from?	Hvorfra kommer du?
I'm from ...	Jeg kommer fra ...
How old are you?	Hvor gammel er du?
I'm looking for ...	Jeg leder efter ...
How much is it?	Hvor meget koster
Today	i dag
Tomorrow	i morgen
Day after tomorrow	i overmorgen
In the morning	om morgenen
In the afternoon	om eftermiddagen
In the evening	om aftenen
Early	tidlig

Search engines: **www.bing.com/?cc=dk**, **www.google.dk**, **dk.yahoo.com**
Local news feed (in English): **www.cphpost.dk**, **jp.dk/uknews**

France

President: Nicolas Sarkozy

Population: 63.4 million

Level of trade with UK: "France is the UK's fourth largest export market behind the US, Germany and the Netherlands and the UK's third largest supplier. Exports to France amount to some £20 billion per year and account for nearly 10% of UK visible exports worldwide."
Foreign & Commonwealth Office

Percentage of population with internet: 68.9%

Size of e-commerce market: 44.6 million with internet access, 77% of whom intended to make online purchases in the second half of 2010.

Local domain suffix: .FR

Currency: Euro (€)

Time zone(s): Central European Time (CET), GMT+1

Traditional dish: Crêpe Suzette, a dessert comprised of a crêpe (a form of specially thin pancake) with *buerre Suzette*, which is a sauce of caramelised butter and sugar, orange/tangerine juice, zest, and Grand Marnier or orange Curaçao liqueur on top. Served flambé.

A few key phrases (from www.quintessenial.co.uk)

English	French
Hello	Bonjour
Good evening	Bonsoir
Good night	Bonne niut
Goodbye	Au revoir
Yes	Oui
No	Non
Please	S'il vous plai
Thank you	Merci
You're welcome	Je vous en prie
How are you?	Comment allez-vous?
Fine thanks	Bien merci
What's your name	Comment appelez-vous?
My name is	Je m'appelle
I don't understand	Je ne comprends pas

Search engines: www.bing.com/?cc=fr, www.google.fr, fr.yahoo.com

Local news feed (in English): www.lefigaro.fr/international, www.france24.com/en/france

Germany

Prime Minister/President: Angela Merkel (Chancellor)

Population: 82.5 million

Level of trade with UK: "Germany is the UK's second largest export market worldwide and the largest in Europe. Meanwhile, the UK is the third largest export market for German goods."
Foreign & Commonwealth Office

Percentage of population with internet: 79.1%

Size of e-commerce market: 65.1 million with internet access, 83% of whom intended to make online purchases in the second half of 2010.

Local domain suffix: .DE

Currency: Euro (€)

Time zone(s): Central European Time (CET), GMT+1

Traditional dish: Sausages (there are more than 1,500 different kinds of *wurst* in Germany).

A few key phrases (from www.kwintessential.co.uk and www.about.com):

English	German
Hello	Hallo
Good morning	Guten Morgen
Good day	Guten Tag
Good evening	Giten Abend
Goodbye	Auf Wiedersehen
Bye	Tschüss
Yes	Ja
No	Nein
Where?	Wo?
Why?	Warum?
How?	Wie?
Please	Bitte
You're welcome	Bitte
Excuse me	Entschuldigung
I understand	Ich verstehe
I don't understand	Ich verstehe nicht

Search engines: www.bing.com/?cc=de, www.google.de, de.yahoo.com

Local news feed (in English): www.spiegel.de/international, www.thelocal.de

Greece

Prime Minister: George Papandreou

Population: 10.94 million

Level of trade with UK: "Greece is the UK's 28th largest export market. The value of exports of British goods to Greece was £1.56 billion in 2009, while Greek imports to the UK stood at £527 million."
Foreign & Commonwealth Office

Percentage of population with internet: 46.2%

Size of e-commerce market: 4.9 million with internet access, 77% of whom intended to make online purchases in the second half of 2010.

Local domain suffix: .GR

Currency: Euro (€)

Time zone(s): Eastern European Standard Time (EET), GMT+2

Traditional dish: *Patsas*, or tripe soup. Variants include calf feet instead of tripe. Reputedly a hangover cure as well as an adventurous lunch.

A few key phrases (from www.kwintessential.co.uk):

English	Greek [phonetic]
Hello	yasa
Goodbye	andio
Good morning	kalimera
Good afternoon	herete
Good evening	kalispera
Good night	kalinihta
Please	parakalo
Thank you	efharisto
Yes	ne
No	ohi
Sorry	sighnomi
How are you?	Ti kanete?
I'm well thanks	kala efharisto
What's your name?	pos sas lene
My name is	me lene
Do you speak English?	milate anglika?
I understand	katalaveno
I don't understand	dhen katalaveno
Where is?	pou ine
How much?	poso kani
When?	pote

Search engines: www.google.com.gr, gr.yahoo.com

Local news feed (in English): www.athensnews.gr, www.ekathimerini.com

Hong Kong

Chief Executive: Donald Tsang

Population: 7 million

Level of trade with UK: "Hong Kong is the UK's 12th largest export market worldwide (2009) and the 2nd largest in the Asia Pacific region behind China, but ahead of Japan, India, Singapore and Australia (2009). In 2009 UK exports to Hong Kong were valued at £3.51bn."
Foreign & Commonwealth Office

Percentage of population with internet: 66.8%

Size of e-commerce market: 4.8 million with internet access, 73% of whom intended to make online purchases in the second half of 2010.

Local domain suffix: .HK

Currency: Hong Kong Dollar

Time zone(s): China Standard Time, GMT+8

Traditional dish: Anything Cantonese (a traditional gastronomic saying in Hong Kong used to be "Eat in Canton"), including braised shark fin – a meal once so rarefied that it cost the equivalent of six months' wages of a working class family (but which is now slightly less expensive).

A few key phrases (from www.languagetutoring.co.uk and www.kwintessential.co.uk)

English	Mandarin [Pinyin]
Hello	Ni hao
Goodbye	Zaijian
May I ask your name?	Nin guxing
My name is...	Wo xing
I am from	Wo shi cong...laide
Could you speak more slowly please?	Qing ni shuo man yidian hao ma?
I do not understand	Wo tingbudong
Telephone	dianhua
International call	guoji dianhua
Computer	diannao
Email	dianziyoujian, or just email
Internet	yinte wang/hulian wang
Where can I get online?	Wo zai nar keyi shang wang?
Are there any messages for me?	you meiyou liu hua?

English	Cantonese [Pinyin]
Hello, how are you?	nehih ho ma?
Fine	geih ho
Goodbye	baahih baahih/joih gin
Thanks	M goih
Excuse me	M goih
Do you speak English?	Nehih sik m sik gong ying man a?
I don't understand	Ngoh m mihng

Search engines: www.bing.com/?cc=hk, www.google.hk, hk.yahoo.com

Local news feed (in English): www.thestandard.com.hk, www.scmp.com

India

Prime Minister: Manmohan Singh

Population: 1.17 billion

Level of trade with UK: "Bilateral trade between the UK and India is £12.6 billion (2008)."
UKTI

Percentage of population with internet: 6.9%

Size of e-commerce market: 81 million with internet access. Statistics on purchaser intent were not available.

Local domain suffix: .IN

Currency: Rupee

Time zone(s): India Standard Time (IST), GMT+5.30

Traditional dish: India specialises in flat breads, including *Appam, dosa, roti, paratha, kulcha, naan* and *uttapam.* Not to mention deep-fried breads such as *puri* and *bhatoora.* Dough is primarily from milled flour, though some are also stuffed with vegetables and interlarded with *ghee* or butter; Indian batter is made typically from ingredients such as rice and black lentils.

A few key phrases (from www.kwintessential.co.uk):

English	Hindi [phonetic]
Hello/goodbye	namaste
Excuse me	maaf kijiyeh
Please	meharbani she
Thank you	shukriya
Yes	haan
No	nahin
How are you?	aap kiaseh hain?
Very well, thank you	bahut acha, shukriya
What's your name?	aap ka shubh naam kya hai?
My name is	meraa naam hai
Do you speak English?	Kya aap angrezi aatee hai?
I don't understand	meri samajh mei nahin aaya

English	Bangla (Bengali) [phonetic]
Hello (Muslim)	asalaam alaykum
Hello (Hindu)	nomaashkaar
Goodbye	khudaa hafiz
See you later	pore dakhaa hobe
Excuse me	maaf korun
Yes	ji
No	naa
No problem	tik aache
How are you?	kaamon aachen?

Search engines: www.bing.com/?cc=in, www.google.in, in.yahoo.com

Local news feed (in English): www.hindustantimes.com, timesofindia.indiatimes.com

Ireland (Eire)

Prime Minister: Brian Cowen (Taoiseach)

Population: 4.2 million

Level of trade with UK: "Two-way trade in goods and services amounted to more than £43 billion in 2008 (the latest year for which service figures are available) At £15.2 billion, Ireland is still the UK's fifth largest export market."
Foreign & Commonwealth Office

Percentage of population with internet: 65.8%

Size of e-commerce market: 3.04 million with internet access, 83% of whom intended to make online purchases in the second half of 2010. Local domain suffix: .IE

Currency: Euro (€)

Time zone(s): Greenwich Mean Time (GMT)

Traditional dish: Irish stew – beef, lamb (or mutton), admixed with potatoes, onions, parsley and carrots. More modern recipes also call for Guinness.

Ireland has two official languages, English and Irish (or 'Gaeilge' as it is commonly known). Road signs, street names, public bathroom facilities, etc. may show names in both languages.

A few key phrases (from www.tripadvisor.com):

English	Irish
Hello	Dia Duit
How are you?	Conas atá tú?
Thank you	Go raibh maith agat
Good luck	Go n'éirí an bóthar leat
Goodbye	Slán
Cheers!	Sláinte!

Search engines: www.bing.com/?cc=ie, www.google.ie, ie.yahoo.com

Local news feed: www.irishtimes.com, www.independent.ie

Italy

Prime Minister: Silvio Berlusconi

Population: 60 million

Level of trade with UK: "UK exports to Italy in 2008 were valued at over £9 billion and imports from Italy were over £13 billion. Despite the economic crisis, trade in 2009 [was] on a par with 2008."
Foreign & Commonwealth Office

Percentage of population with internet: 51.7%

Size of e-commerce market: 30 million with internet access, 78% of whom intended to make online purchases in the second half of 2010.

Local domain suffix: .IT

Currency: Euro (€)

Time zone(s): Central European Time (CET), GMT+1

Traditional dish: Anything from Parma (for example, a *savarin di riso* – a kind of risotto wrapped in ham). Italy legally blocked a number of EU developments until it was assured that EFSA (the European Food Safety Authority) would be based out of this "poco capitale" (little capital), the home of prosciutto and parmesan cheese (of which over 2 million tons are sold annually). Pizza and pasta are also popular.

A few key phrases (from www.smartphrase.com):

English	Italian
Please	Per piacere / Per favore
Thank you (very much)	(Mille) grazie
Excuse me	Mi scusi
I'm sorry, but...	Mi spiace, ma...
That's a shame	E' un peccato!
May I... ?	Posso... ?
Take care!	Stai (stia) attento
Have a nice day!	Buona giornata!
Yes	Si
No	No
I think so	Io penso di sì
It doesn't matter	Non importa
I don't mind	Mi è indifferente
Of course	Ovviamente
True	É vero
With pleasure	Con piacere

Search engines: www.bing.com/?cc=it, www.google.it, it.yahoo.com

Local news feed (in English): www.corriere.it/english, www.ansa.it/web/notizie/rubriche/english/english.shtml

Japan

Prime Minister: Naoto Kan

Population: 126.6 million

Level of trade with UK: "Japan is the UK's largest export market after Europe, China, the US, Hong Kong and Dubai, and Britain is Japan's ninth largest market ... The UK exported about £8.9 billion of goods and services to Japan in 2008/09."
Foreign & Commonwealth Office

Percentage of population with internet: 78.2%

Size of e-commerce market: 99 million with internet access, 80% of whom intended to make online purchases in the second half of 2010.

Local domain suffix: .JP

Currency: Yen (¥)

Time zone(s): Japan Standard Time (JST), GMT+9

Traditional dish: Curry, but with a difference. Curry was first introduced to Japan by the British, via India, in the Meiji modernisation of the 19th century. It has since taken on a distinct Japanese style, notably using honey and apples as key ingredients. Sushi, sashimi, tempura and noodles are other popular choices.

Go Global

A few key phrases (from www.ukti.gov.uk):

English	Japanese
Good morning (used up to about 10am)	Ohayou gozaimasu
Hello / Good day (used from about 10am)	Konnichiwa
Good evening	Konbanwa
Good night	Oyasumi nasai
Goodbye	Sayounara
Excuse me	Sumimasen
I am sorry	Gomen nasai
Thank you	Arigatou
Yes (I've heard you)	Hai
No	Iie

Search engines: www.bing.com/?cc=jp, www.google.jp, www.yahoo.co.jp

Local news feed (in English): www.japantimes.co.jp, www.japantoday.com

Luxembourg

Prime Minister: Jean-Claude Juncker

Population: 500,000

Level of trade with UK: "UK exports to Luxembourg went down from €360 million in 2000 to €237 million in 2009 (average over this period €569 million) whilst imports from Luxembourg went down by 29% to €405 million (2000: €572 million, average €569 million). The import-export balance was negative for goods in 2009 (-€3,014 million) and positive in services (€17,996 million)."
Foreign & Commonwealth Office

Percentage of population with internet: 85.3%

Size of e-commerce market: 424,500 with internet access. Statistics on purchase intent are unavailable.

Local domain suffix: .LU

Currency: Euro (€)

Time zone(s): Central European Time (CET), GMT+1

Traditional dish: *Judd Mat Gaardebou'nen*: soaked collar of pork with broad beans. Reportedly boasting more Michelin stars per inhabitant than any other country on earth, Luxembourgers may not ever actually cook this themselves.

Go Global

A few key phrases (from www.expatica.lu):

Luxembourgish	English
Yes	Jo
No	Neen
Maybe	Vläicht
Hello	Moien
Good morning	Gudde Moien
Good afternoon	Gudde Mëtteg
Good evening	Gudden Owend
Goodbye	Äddi
Thank you	Merci
Why?	Firwat?
I don't know	Ech weess net
I don't understand	Ech verstinn net
Excuse me?	Watgelift? or Entschëllegt?
Do you speak German/French/English?	Schwätzt dir Däitsch/Franséisch/Englesch?
What is your name?	Wéi heeschs du?
How are you?	Wéi geet et?

Search engines: www.bing.com/?cc=lu, www.google.lu

Local news feed (in Luxembourgish): www.wort.lu, www.station.lu

Netherlands, The

Prime Minister: Jan-Peter Balkenende

Population: 16.5 million

Level of trade with UK: "The Netherlands is the UK's third largest bilateral trading partner at £38bn in 2007; our third largest export market globally (behind only the US and Germany) and our second largest within the EU. Total exports [from the UK to Netherlands] in 2007 equalled £14.9bn."
Foreign & Commonwealth Office

Percentage of population with internet: 88.6%

Size of e-commerce market: 14.9 million with internet access. Statistics on purchase intent are unavailable.

Local domain suffix: .NL

Currency: Euro (€)

Time zone(s): Central European Time (CET), GMT+1

Traditional dish: *Stamppot rauwe andijvie*: raw endive (a leaf vegetable related to daisies) mashed with hot potatoes and served with diced fried speck (a form of bacon).

Go Global

A few key phrases (from www.kwintessential.co.uk):

English	Dutch
Hello	Dag/Hallo
Goodbye	Dag
See you soon	Tat ziens
Yes	Ja
No	Nee
Please	Alstublieft
Thank you	Dank u
Excuse me	Pardon
How are you?	Hoe gaat het met u/jou?
I'm fine thanks	Goed, bedankt.
My name is	Ik heet
Where are you from?	Waar komt u/kom je vandaan?
I'm from	Ik kom uit
Do you speak English?	Spreekt u/Spreek je Engels?
I don't understand	Ik begrijp het niet

Most popular search engine: www.bing.com/?cc=nl, nl.yahoo.com, www.google.nl

Local news feed (in English): www.dutchnews.nl

Norway

Prime Minister: Jens Stoltenberg

Population: 4.8 million

Level of trade with UK: "The UK is Norway's largest export market with a total value of £20,646 billion in 2008. This figure reflects the fact that over 70% of gas imported by the UK is piped directly from Norway. Norway is an important export market for the UK with a total value in 2008 of £2.76 billion."
Foreign & Commonwealth Office

Percentage of population with internet: 94.8%

Size of e-commerce market: 4.4 million with internet access, 89% of whom intended to make online purchases in the second half of 2010.

Local domain suffix: .NO

Currency: Norwegian Krone

Time zone(s): Central European Time (CET), GMT+1

Traditional dish: Smoked salmon, a dish in fact originating from this country. Often served with scrambled eggs, or eaten raw.

Go Global

A few key phrases (from www.omniglot.com):

English	Norweigan
Hello	Goddag / Hei / Morn, Hallo (on phone)
How are you?	Hvordan har du det?
I'm fine, thanks. And you?	(Jo) takk bare bra. Og du?
Long time no see	Lenge siden sist! Det er lenge siden sist vi møttes!
What's your name?	Hva heter du? Kva heiter du?
My name is ...	Jeg heter ... (Bokmål); Eg heiter ... (Nynorsk)
Where are you from?	Hvor er du fra? (Bokmål); Kvar kjem du frå? Kvar er du frå? (Nynorsk)
I'm from ...	Jeg er fra ... (Bokmål) Eg kjem frå ... / Eg er frå ...(Nynorsk)
Pleased to meet you	Hyggelig å møte deg / Artig å treffe deg
Good morning	God morgen
Good afternoon	God ettermiddag
How much is this?	Hva koster denne/dette?
Sorry	Beklager, Unnskyld
Please	Vær så snill
Thank you	Takk (thanks) Tusen Takk (a thousand thanks); Mange Takk (many thanks); Takk så mye (thanks a lot)

Search engines: www.bing.com/?cc=no, www.google.no, no.yahoo.com

Local news feed (in English): www.norwaypost.no, www.norwaynews.com/en

Poland

President: Lech Kaczynski

Population: 38.1 million

Level of trade with UK: "In 2008, the UK retained its position as Poland's fourth largest trading partner and Poland remained the UK's largest export market in Central and Eastern Europe."
Foreign & Commonwealth Office

Percentage of population with internet: 58.4%

Size of e-commerce market: 22.4 million with internet access, 84% of whom intended to make online purchases in the second half of 2010.

Local domain suffix: .PL

Currency: Zloty

Time zone(s): Central European Time (CET), GMT+1

Traditional dish: Try *ozór wolowy* (soft steamed beef tongues). If less adventurous, *zrazy zawijane*, a kind of Polish progenitor of the hamburger (itself an invention from neighbouring Germany) – beef rolls stuffed with bacon, gherkin and onion or red pepper, in a spicy sauce.

Go Global

A few key phrases (from the BBC's h2G2):

English	Polish
Hello	Witam (formal) / Czesc (informal)
Good morning/day	Dzien dobry
Good evening	Dobry wieczór
Excuse me / I'm sorry	Przepraszam
Please	Prosze
Thank you	Dziekuje
You're welcome	Prosze bardzo
I don't understand	Nie rozumiem
Yes	Tak
No	Nie
Open	Otwarte/Czynne
Closed	Zamkniete

Search engines: **www.bing.com/?cc=pl**, **www.google.pl**

Local news feed (in English): **www.thenews.pl**, **www.nwe.pl**

Portugal

Prime Minister: José Sócrates

Population: 10.6 million

Level of trade with UK: "Links between the two countries have always been strong and bilateral trade is worth over £3bn. In 2008, UK exports to Portugal totalled £1.6bn, and UK imports from Portugal totalled £1.7bn."
Foreign & Commonwealth Office

Percentage of population with internet: 48.1%

Size of e-commerce market: 5.1 million with internet access, 69% of whom intended to make online purchases in the second half of 2010.

Local domain suffix: .PT

Currency: Euro (€)

Time zone(s): Western European Time (WET), GMT

Traditional dish: *Francesinha*, a sandwich covered in molten cheese and tomato and beer sauce, filled with either ham, sausages, steak or some other roast meat, and served with chips. Reputedly an attempt to adapt the French croque-monsieur to Portuguese tastes, it does so largely by turning it half inside out and dousing it in warm alcoholic sauce.

A few key phrases (from www.kwintessential.co.uk):

English	Portuguese
Hello	Bom dia
Good morning	Bom dia
Good evening	Boa tarde
Goodbye	Adeus
Yes/No	Sim/Não
Maybe	Talvez
Please	Se faz favour/Por favor
Thank you	Obrigado/a
You're welcome	De nada
Excuse me	Desculpe
Beautiful	belo
Better	melhor
Excellent	excelente
Good	bom/boa
Happy	feliz
Ill	doente
One more/another	mais um(a)

Search engines: www.bing.com/?cc=pt, www.google.com.pt

Local news feed (in English): www.portugal.com/news, www.the-news.net

Russia

President: Dmitri Medvedev

Population: 141.9 million

Level of trade with UK: "Trade between the UK and Russia has been growing at around 25% annually for the last five years ... Russia is the UK's 22nd largest export market ... [though] exports of UK goods were valued at £2.3bn in 2009, substantially down as a result of the Russian recession and falling demand for luxury imports, particularly automobiles."
Foreign & Commonwealth Office

Percentage of population with internet: 42.8%

Size of e-commerce market: 59.7 million with internet access, 79% of whom intended to make online purchases in the second half of 2010.

Local domain suffix: .RU

Currency: Rouble

Time zone(s): Moscow Standard Time (MST), GMT+3. St Petersburg and Moscow share this time zone, but there are a total of nine time zones across the Russian federation.

Traditional dish: Russian Salad, also called *Salade Olivier* – meat, boiled and diced vegetables and potatoes, bound in mayonnaise and served cold. Invented by Lucien Olivier in the 1860s, its original recipe was closely guarded, but various attempts at the time to narrow it down helpfully confirmed that it contained: caviar, grouse, tongue of veal, crayfish tails, smoked duck and capers. Since then, it has variously been said to also include sausage, truffles, lobster meat, anchovy fillets and ham. Most modern variations include only sausage, potatoes and vegetables.

A few key phrases (from www.kwintessential.co.uk):

English	Russian [phonetic]
My name is ...	min-ya za-voot
What is your name?	kak vas za-voot
Pleased to meet you	och-en pree-yat-na
Thank you	spa-see-ba
Please/You're welcome	pa-zhal-sta
Yes	da
No	nyet
Goodbye	da-svee-da-nee-ye

Search engines: www.bing.com/?cc=ru, www.google.ru, ru.yahoo.com

Local news feed (in English): www.themoscowtimes.com

Saudi Arabia

Head of State and Prime Minister: King Abdullah bin Abdul Aziz Al Saud

Population: 25.7 million

Level of trade with UK: "The UK's export of goods to Saudi Arabia amounted to £2.19 billion in 2008. Exports of services totalled £2.65 billion, with income and current transfers adding another £1.73 billion."
UKTI

Percentage of population with internet: 38.1%

Size of e-commerce market: 9.8 million with internet access, around two-thirds of whom intended to make online purchases in the second half of 2010.

Local domain suffix: .SA

Currency: Saudi Riyal

Time zone(s): GMT+3

Traditional dish: Laban, a kind of traditional Saudi smoothie: half a cup of plain yoghurt, half a cup of ice water and a handful of ice cubs. Blended these days, but stirred in the past.

A few key phrases (from www.kwintessential.co.uk):

English	Saudi Arabian [phonetic]
Hello	Marhaba
How are you?	Keef Halek
Good morning	Sabah Al Kair
Good evening	Masaa Al Kair
Good	Kowaies
Very good	Kowaies Kateer
Please	Min Fadlak
Thank you	Shoo kran
Excuse me	Ismahlee
Never mind	Maa leesh
OK	Taieb
Yes	Aiwa
No	La
Maybe	Yimken
None, nothing, nobody	Mafee

Search engines: www.bing.com/?cc=sa, www.google.com.sa

Local news feed (in English): www.arabnews.com, www.alarabiya.net

Singapore

Prime Minister: Lee Hsien Loong

Population: 4.84m

Level of trade with UK: "Nearly two-thirds of all UK exports of goods and services to Southeast Asia [were] to Singapore in 2008. Outside of Europe, Singapore is the UK's sixth largest export market and seventh largest source of imports."
Foreign & Commonwealth Office

Percentage of population with internet: 77.8%

Size of e-commerce market: 3.6 million with internet access. Statistics on purchaser intent were not available.

Local domain suffix: .SG

Currency: Singapore Dollar

Time zone(s): Singapore Standard Time (SST), GMT+8

Traditional dish: Fish head curry. Not the hideous potage of *Beano* school dinners, but a dish fusing Indian, Chinese and Malay influences, and generally comprised of the head of a red snapper, stewed in curry and vegetables and served with rice or bread.

Search engines: www.bing.com/?cc=sg, www.google.sg, sg.yahoo.com

Local news feed (in English): www.straitstimes.com

South Africa

President: Jacob Zuma

Population: 48.7 million

Level of trade with UK: "The UK is one of South Africa's most significant trading partners, with over £8 billion in two-way trade in goods and services."
Foreign & Commonwealth Office

Percentage of population with internet: 10.8%

Size of e-commerce market: 5.3 million with internet access, 66% of whom intended to make online purchases in the second half of 2010. Across Africa, 47% of those with internet access have never made an online purchase.

Local domain suffix: .ZA

Currency: Rand

Time zone(s): GMT+2

Traditional dish: Boerwors sausages: beef and pork mince, with nutmeg and coriander, best served with monkey gland sauce. (Vinegar, brown sugar, Tabasco, Worcester sauce, pepper, garlic, chilli, mustard powder, red wine, tomato ketchup, port, onions and curry powder. Less is decidedly more.)

Search engines: www.google.co.za

Local news feed (in English): www.mg.co.za, www.todayszaman.com

South Korea

President: Lee Myung-bak

Population: 48.7 million

Level of trade with UK: "With a predicted economic growth rate of 5% in 2010, this makes South Korea the 4th largest economy in Asia and the 14th globally. With the introduction of the EU/South Korea Free Trade Agreement and a passion for UK goods, South Korea is becoming a lucrative market with numerous and varied opportunities."
UKTI

Percentage of population with internet: 81.1%

Size of e-commerce market: 39.4 million with internet access, 95% of whom intended to make online purchases in the second half of 2010.

Local domain suffix: .KR

Currency: ROK Won

Time zone(s): South Korea Time (SKT), GMT+9

Traditional dish: Marinated crabs – *gejang*. Crustacean flesh soaked in soy sauce or chilli pepper powder. Bundles of live crabs may be purchased for this purpose from Korean markets, in the form of long plaits of straw with a dozen or more writhing creatures attached by coloured ribbons.

English is the common language of business in Korea.

Search engines: **www.google.kr, kr.yahoo.com**

Local news feed (in English): **www.koreaherald.com**

Spain

Prime Minister: Jose Luis Rodriguez Zapatero

Population: 44.6 million

Level of trade with UK: "Spain is the UK's seventh largest export market. In 2008 exports (good & services) were valued at £15.7bn, and Spain [was the UK's] 8th largest import source (£21.4bn)." *Foreign & Commonwealth Office*

Percentage of population with internet: 62.6%

Size of e-commerce market: 29 million with internet access, 72% of whom intended to make online purchases in the second half of 2010.

Local domain suffix: .ES

Currency: Euro (€)

Time zone(s): Central European Time (CET), GMT+1

Traditional dish: Paella, of which there are three forms – perhaps the most daring being 'freestyle', or *estilo libre*, which combines seafood *and* meat (sometimes snails), vegetables, beans, along with the usual calasparra or bomba rices, saffron and olive oil.

A few key phrases (from www.smartphrase.com):

English	Spanish
Please	Por favor
Thank you (very much)	(Muchas) Gracias
Excuse me	¡Perdone!
I'm sorry, but...	Lo siento, pero...
That's a shame	Es una lástima
May I... ?	¿Puedo...?
Yes	Sí
No	No
That depends	Depende
I don't know	No lo sé
I don't think so	Creo que no
I think so	Creo que sí
It doesn't matter	No importa
I don't mind	No me molesta
Of course!	¡Claro!
True	Es verdad
With pleasure	Con gust

Search engines: www.bing.com/?cc=es, www.google.es, es.yahoo.com

Local news feed (in English): www.spanishnews.es, www.typicallyspanish.com

Sweden

Prime Minister: Fredrik Reinfeldt

Population: 9.1 million

Level of trade with UK: "Sweden is the UK's tenth largest export market and the UK is Sweden's third largest supplier."
Foreign & Commonwealth Office

Percentage of population with internet: 92.5%

Size of e-commerce market: 8.3 million with internet access, 78% of whom intended to make online purchases in the second half of 2010.

Local domain suffix: .SE

Currency: Swedish Krona (SEK)

Time zone(s): Central European Time (CET), GMT+1

Traditional dish: Meatballs, which traditionally ought to be half an inch in diameter; served with gravy, potatoes and lingonberry jam (which is also eaten on toast, and sold in IKEA superstores in special bucket containers).

A few key phrases (from www.kwintessential.co.uk):

English	Swedish
Hello	Hej
Goodbye	Adjö/Hej då
Yes	Ja
No	Nej
Please	Snälla/Vänligen
Thank you	Tack
That's fine	Det är bra
You are welcome	Varsågod
Excuse me (Sorry)	Ursäkta mig/Förlåt
Do you speak English?	Talar du engelska?

Search engines: www.bing.com/?cc=se, www.google.se, se.yahoo.com

Local news feed (in English): www.thelocal.se, www.stockholmnews.com

Switzerland

President: Doris Leuthard

Population: 7.7 million

Level of trade with UK: "In 2009 Switzerland was the UK's third largest non-EU market after the US and China, with goods exports totalling more than £3.9bn. Swiss consumers buy, on average, more British products than their French or German neighbours." *Foreign & Commonwealth Office*

Percentage of population with internet: 75.3%

Size of e-commerce market: 5.7 million with internet access, 83% of whom intended to make online purchases in the second half of 2010.

Local domain suffix: .CH

Currency: Swiss franc (CHF)

Time zone(s): Central European Time (CET), GMT+1

Traditional dish/food: Chocolate. Though outlawed in Zurich in the 1700s owing to its purported qualities as an aphrodisiac, the Swiss now consume more chocolate per capita than any other nation.

A few key phrases: See France and Germany.

Search engines: www.bing.com/?cc=ch, www.google.ch, ch.yahoo.com

Local news feed (in German): www.baz.ch

Turkey

President: Abdullah Gul

Population: 71.9 million

Level of trade with UK: "The overall volume of UK-Turkey bilateral trade reached $14.8 billion [approx £9.5bn] in 2008."
Foreign & Commonwealth Office

Percentage of population with internet: 45%

Size of e-commerce market: 35 million with internet access, 72% of whom intended to make online purchases in the second half of 2010.

Local domain suffix: .TR

Currency: Turkish Lira

Time zone(s): Eastern European Standard Time (EET), GMT+2

Traditional dish: Börek – filled pastries, made from thin *yufka* dough, and fried. Fillings and shape vary across all the regions of the former Ottoman Empire, and take in everything from spicy mincemeat to citrus fruits and sugar.

Go Global

A few key phrases (from www.business-with-turkey.com):

English	Turkish
Good evening	iyi aksamlar
Good morning	günaydın
Good night	iyi geceler
Hello	merhaba
How are you?	nasılsınız?
How much?	ne kadar?
No	hayır
Please	lütfen
Yes	evet
Cash against goods	mal mukabili
Cash against documents	vesaik mukabili
Letter of credit	akreditif
Cash up front	pesin ödeme

Search engines: www.bing.com/?cc=tr, www.google.com.tr, tr.yahoo.com

Local news feed (in English): www.hurriyetdailynews.com, www.todayszaman.com

United Arab Emirates (including Dubai)

Head of State: Sheikh Khalifa Bin Zayed al-Nahyan

Population: 4.6 million

Level of trade with UK: "The UAE is [the UK's] largest trading partner in the Middle East (£2.3 billion in 2007, though the latest figures, still pending, are likely to be much higher)."
Foreign & Commonwealth Office

Percentage of population with internet: 75.9%

Size of e-commerce market: 3.7 million with internet access, 66% of whom intended to make online purchases in the second half of 2010.

Local domain suffix: .AE

Currency: UAE Dirham

Time zone(s): GMT+4

Traditional dish: Shawarma, a wrap of shaved lamb and chicken (meat cut away on a rotisserie, not animals that have met a Gillette razor).

English is the common language used in business.

Search engines: www.bing.com/?cc=ae, www.google.ae

Local news feed (in English): www.thenational.ae, www.gulfnews.com

USA

President: Barack Obama

Population: 307 million

Level of trade with UK: "The United States is the UK's top export destination and its second-largest trading partner overall (after Germany) for goods, reaching a record $112 billion in 2008. The UK is the US's largest trading partner for services, worth $110 billion in 2008."
Foreign & Commonwealth Office

Percentage of population with internet: 77.3%

Size of e-commerce market: 220.1 million with internet access, 80% of whom intended to make online purchases in the second half of 2010.

Local domain suffix: .US

Currency: US dollar ($)

Time zone(s): Eastern (GMT-5), Central (GMT-6), Mountain (GMT-7) and Pacific (GMT-8).

Traditional dish: Burger and fries. German and French in origin, respectively, this has nevertheless become the favoured dish of presidents and public alike. Barack Obama most recently ate a cheeseburger with the president of Russia. They shared their fries.

Search engines: www.bing.com, www.google.com, www.yahoo.com

Local news feed: www.bloomberg.com, www.nytimes.com, online.wsj.com

Appendix 2:
International trade bodies for
the UK's top 30 export nations

Europe

Belgium
Belgian Chamber of Commerce: www.blcc.co.uk

Czech Republic
Czech British Chamber of Commerce: www.cbcc.org.uk

Denmark
The Danish-UK Chamber of Commerce: www.ducc.co.uk

France
French Chamber of Commerce in the UK: www.ccfgb.co.uk

Germany
German British Chamber of Commerce: grossbritannien.ahk.de

Greece
British Hellenic Chamber of Commerce: www.bhcc.gr

Ireland
Enterprise Ireland: www.enterprise-ireland.com

Italy
Italian Chamber of Commerce and Industry for the UK:
www.italchamind.eu

Netherlands, The
The Netherlands British Chamber of Commerce: www.nbcc.co.uk

Norway
Norwegian-British Chamber of Commerce:
www.norwegian-chamber.co.uk

Poland
British Polish Chamber of Commerce: www.bpcc.org.pl

Portugal
Portuguese Chamber: www.portuguese-chamber.org.uk

Russia
Russo-British Chamber of Commerce: www.rbcc.com

Spain
Spanish Chamber of Commerce in Great Britain:
www.spanishchamber.co.uk

Sweden
Swedish Chamber of Commerce for the UK: www.scc.org.uk

Switzerland
The British Swiss Chamber of Commerce www.bscc.co.uk

Turkey
Turkish-British Chamber of Commerce and Industry:
www.tbcci.org

Australasia

Australia
Austrade: www.austrade.gov.au

Asia

Hong Kong
Hong Kong Trade Development Council: www.hktdc.com

Japan
Japan External Trade Organization (JETRO): www.jetro.go.jp

China
China-Britain Business Council: www.cbbc.org

India
UK India Business Council: www.ukibc.com

Singapore
EnterpriseOne: www.business.gov.sg

South Korea
Korea Business Centre London: www.kotra.org.uk

Africa

South Africa
British Chamber of Business in Southern Africa:
www.britishchamber.co.za

North America

Canada
High Commission of Canada in the UK:
www.canadainternational.gc.ca/united_kingdom-royaume_uni

USA
BritishAmerican Business: www.babinc.org

South America

Brazil
Embassy of Brazil in London: www.brazil.org.uk/economy

Middle East

Dubai
Dubai Chamber of Commerce: www.dubaicity.com/government-departments/dubai-chamber-of-commerce-and-industry.htm

Appendix 3:
Customs declaration forms

Copy of CN22 declaration

CUSTOMS DECLARATION DÉCLARATION EN DOUANE	CN 22
	May be opened officially Peut être ouvert d'office

Great Britain\Grande-Bretagne   **Important!**   **See instructions on the back**

	Gift\Cadeau		Commercial sample\Echantillon commercial
	Documents		Other\Autre *Tick one or more boxes*

Quantity and detailed description of contents (1) Quantité et description détaillée du contenu	Weight (*in kg*)(2) Poids	Value (3) Valeur

For commercial items only If known, HS tariff number (4) and country of origin of goods (5) *N°tarifaire du SH et pays d'origine des marchandises (si connus)*	Total Weight Poids total (*in kg*) (6)	Total Value (7) Valeur totale

I, the undersigned, whose name and address are given on the item, certify that the particulars given in this declaration are correct and that this item does not contain any dangerous article or articles prohibited by legislation or by postal or customs regulations

Date and sender's signature (8)

Available for download at:

ftp.royalmail.com/Downloads/public/ctf/rm/cn22.pdf

Copy of CN23 declaration

From De	Great Britain Grande-Bretagne		Sender's Customs reference (if any) Référence en douane de l'expéditeur (si elle existe)	CUSTOMS DECLARATION	CN 23
	Name			No. of item (barcode, if any) | May be opened officially	Important!
	Business			DÉCLARATION EN DOUANE	See instructions on the back
	Street			N° de l'envoi (code à barres, s'il existe) | Peut être ouvert d'office	
	Postcode City				
	Country				
To A	Name				
	Business				
	Street			Importer's reference (if any) (tax code/VAT No./importer code) (optional) Référence de l'importateur (si elle existe (code fiscal/N° de TVA/code de l'importateur) (facultatif)	
	Postcode City			Importer's telephone/fax/e-mail (if known)	
	Country			N° de telephone/fax/e-mail de l'importateur (si connus)	

Detailed description of contents (1) Description détaillée du contenu	Quantity (2) Quantité	Net Weight (3) Poids Net (in kg)	Value (5) Valeur	For commercial items only Pour les envois commercial seulement	
				HS tariff number (7) N° tarifaire du SH	Country of origin of goods (8) Pays d'origine des marchandises
		Total gross weight (4) Poids brut total	Total value (6) Valeur totale	Postal charges/Fees (9) Frais de port/Frais	

Category of item (10) Catégorie de l'envoi	Commercial sample Échantillon commercial Explanation: Explication:	Office of origin/Date of posting Bureau d'origine/Date de dépôt
☐ Gift Cadeau	☐ Returned goods Retour de marchandise	
☐ Documents	☐ Other Autre	

Comments (11): (e.g.: goods subject to quarantine, sanitary/phytosanitary inspection or other restrictions)
Observations: (p. ex. Marchandise soumise à la quarantaine/à des contrôles sanitaires, phytosanitaires ou à d'autres restrictions)

I certify that the particulars given in this customs declaration are correct and that this item does not contain any dangerous article or articles prohibited by legislation or by postal or customs regulations

☐ Licence (12) Licence No(s). of licence(s)	☐ Certificate (13) Certificat No(s). of certificate(s)	☐ Invoice (14) Facture No. of invoice	Date and sender's signature (15)

Available for download at:

ftp.royalmail.com/Downloads/public/ctf/rm/CN23.pdf

Appendix 4: World time zones

To check an international time now, visit
www.timeanddate.com/worldclock

London
Mon 09.00

New York
Mon 04.00

Paris
Mon 10.00

Tokyo
Mon 17.00

Stockholm
Mon 10.00

San Francisco
Mon 0 1.00

Dubai
Mon 12.00

Abu Dhabi
Mon 12.00

Berlin
Mon 10.00

Lima	**Dublin**	**Oslo**
Mon 03.00	Mon 09.00	Mon 10.00
Sydney	**Auckland**	**Beijing**
Mon 19.00	Mon 21.00	Mon 16.00
Shanghai	**Delhi**	**Bangalore**
Mon 16.00	Mon 13.30	Mon 13.30
Johannesburg	**Athens**	**Milan**
Mon 10.00	Mon 11.00	Mon 10.00

Appendix 5:
Cultural briefing

Here are a few pointers to bear in mind in countries across Europe, the Middle East and Asia. Advice was taken from Jessica Houghton of Expert Language Solutions and sourced from language/cultural site www.kwintessential.co.uk.

China

Chinese people are very patriotic, so never criticise China or the Chinese government, not even in small talk. In business card exchange, the card is presented with two hands and the body bowed forward slightly to demonstrate your respect to each other and to signal a good start to the business relationship. Chinese people are very superstitious; giving a clock as a gift to a potential client in China would be committing a faux pas, since a clock or a watch also symbolises death. On the contrary, the number 'eight' is very lucky. Superstition is often a determining factor in business decision-making.

India

The handshake can be used but more traditional is the *namaste*, with palms brought together and the head bowed. Indian society has an aversion to saying "no" – it is considered rude due to the possibility of causing disappointment or offence. Listen carefully to responses to your questions. If terms such as "We'll see", "I will try" or "possibly" are employed, then the chances are that, without saying it, they are saying 'no'!

Russia

Russians are transactional and do not need to establish long-standing personal relationships before they do business with people. Saying that, it is a good idea to develop a network of people who you know and trust. The Russian word "svyasi" means connections and refers to having friends in high places, which is often required to cut through red tape. Business appointments are necessary and should be made as far in advance as possible. Confirm the meeting when you arrive in the country and again a day or two in advance, avoiding the first week of May, which contains several public holidays.

Saudi Arabia/Yemen

Muslims pray five times per day. Daily routines, appointments and meetings must therefore be fitted in appropriately around prayer times. Friday is the most important religious day and nobody works. Try not to do business during Ramadan (which typically starts in August) as general business activity is reduced. The roles of men and women are far more defined in the Arab culture. Men should not always expect to shake hands with women and should avoid touch and prolonged eye contact.

Spain

Spaniards are a warm, friendly and outgoing people. Face-to-face meetings are important and humour plays a big part in meetings and discussions. But be careful not to use British sarcasm – it may get lost in translation!

Sweden

Swedes are egalitarian in nature, humble and find boasting unacceptable. In many ways, Swedes prefer to listen to others as opposed to ensuring that their own voice is heard. When speaking, Swedes speak softly and calmly. Behaviours in Sweden are strongly balanced towards 'lagom' or 'everything in moderation'.

Index

A

agents and distributors 95-6
Alibaba.com 7, 24, 77, 78-9, 158-9
Amazon Marketplace 77, 85
app development 37-8
Australia 170

B

banks 103
Belgium 171-2
bitsythis.com 93, 121, 139
building a business framework
    selling a product 55
    selling a service 56
blogging (web logging) 34-5
    adding e-commerce 68
    providers
        Blogger 34-5
        Posterous 43
        Wordpress 34-5, 43
Brazil 173-4
British Chambers of Commerce
    157-8
Business Link 12, 95, 113, 119, 121
Business Wire 57

C

Cameron, David 8-9
concerns over going global (and
    the realities) 16-17
crisis of confidence 10-11
    fears and realities 16-17
Canada 175
checklists
    export admin 121
    international mail 105-6
    promotion 66
China 176-7
cultural briefing 231-2
currency brokers 103
currency converter 102
current affairs 58-9
customer service
    answering questions 123-4
    manage projects 125-6
    meetings and calls 124-5
customs declaration forms 227-8
Czech Republic 178-9

D

data lists 74
Denmark 180-1
DHL 107-108
Digital nations, top 20 by internet
    usage 26

Distance Selling Regulations 120-1

domains (websites) 129

    website domains in non-Latin characters 129

E

eBay 7, 80-4,

    international trading guide 84

    top export sales categories 80

e-commerce

    growth 3-4

Elance.com 85

etiquette, cultural and business 140, 231-2

Etsy ix, 16, 42, 85, 86-7, 106-7

export documentation 116-17, 227, 228

Export Marketing Research Scheme (EMRS) 31

export(s)

    duty and tax guidance 119

    insurance 120

    intellectual property and 119

    legalities 118

    proof of 117

    tax treatment 117

F

Facebook 28, 37, 43-4, 47

fears and realities (of going global) 16-17

fiverr.com 88

Flickr 52-3, 132

France 182-3

fulfilment *see* outsourced order fulfilment

G

Germany 184-5

Getting British Business Online 70

'*Go Global*' survey 14, 16-17, 68, 100, 104

Google

    AdWords 41

    Analytics 24, 67, 78

    Checkout 101

    Getting British Business Online 70

    Export Adviser 25

    Profit Calculator 27

government

    how it can help further 18-19

    support 30-1, 60, 151-8

        International Business Wales (IBW) 156-7

        Invest Northern Ireland (INI) 154-6

        UK Trade & Investment (UKTI) 151-3

        Scottish Development International (SDI) 153-4

Greece 186-7

H

Hewlett-Packard (HP) 142-3, 160

    office-in-a-backpack 142-3

Hong Kong 188-9

I

India 190-1

International Business Wales (IBW) 156-7

Invest Northern Ireland (INI) 154-6

Ireland 192

Isle of Man 75-6

iStockphoto 88, 132

Italy 193-4

iTunes 36, 91

    value added tax (VAT) and 91

J

Japan 195-6

L

language(s) 13, 54, 141-2

    most used on the web 134

    translation 130-1

    services

        Applied Language Solutions 131

        Lingo24.com 95, 131

        Wordpress Global Translator 35

    website domains in non-Latin characters 129

    website localisation 128-31

LinkedIn 28, 37, 47, 52, 93

Luxembourg 197-8

M

Market Visit Support (MVS) 61, 152, 155

Marketwire 57

meetings, holding online 124-5

micro publishing, ten routes 34-8

mobile phone sales 73-4

N

Netherlands, The 199-200

Ning 37

Norway 201-202

O

Obama, Barack 8, 222

oDesk.com 94

Ooh.com 94

outsourced order fulfilment 114-15

Overseas Market Introduction Scheme (OMIS) 31

P

Parcelforce 109

payment gateways 100-102

    Checkout 101

    Moneybookers 101-102

    PayPal 71, 100-101, 160-2

        mobile app 74

    RBS Worldpay 101

    Sagepay 102

PayPal 71, 100-101, 160-2

    mobile app 74

podcasting 36, 91

    how to record a podcast 38

Poland 203-4

Portugal 205-6

postage price comparison table 110

postage price comparison tools 27, 109

Powa.com 69, 162-3

press release 57

private sector support 151-164

PR Newswire 57

promotion checklist 66

R

reasons to *Go Global*

    broadened horizons 9

    diversification and innovation 6

    exchange rates 5

    market opportunity 3-5

    political will 8-9

    technology 6-7

Regus 135-7, 163-4

    Businessworld 144

    top ten virtual office locations 137

research 23-33

    links

        for countries 24-5

        for customers 24-5

    proactive 24-8

    reactive 24

Royal Mail 104-105

    international postage costs tool 27

    local look 139

Russia 207-8

S

Sagepay 102

sales platform sites 77-95

Saudi Arabia 209-10

Scottish Development International (SDI) 153-4

search engine(s) 40

    optimisation (SEO) 39-42, 70, 129, 130, 162 *see* also country profiles

Shipwire.com 144-5, 164

shopping cart providers for websites 70

Singapore 211-12

small and medium enterprises (SMEs) 5, 10, 152

Snapfish 35

social media channels 28, 42

    marketing 47

    measuring your reach 53-4

South Africa 212

South Korea 213-14

Spain 214-15

survey tools 28

Sweden 216-17

Switzerland 218

T

third countries 119

time zones of the world 229

   avoid tragedy 124

   irrelevance of 7

tinypay.me 71

TNT Express 109

trade bodies of foreign nations 223-6

Tradeshow Access Programme (TAP) 60, 61, 63, 152

trade shows, making the most of 61-3

travel cost, calculation tool 27

trendwatching.com 58

Turkey 219-20

Twitter 28, 43, 47-50

   five top apps 48-9

   twenty top international markets 50

U

UKTI *see* UK Trade & Investment (UKTI)

UK Trade & Investment (UKTI) 151-3

United Arab Emirates 221

United States of America (USA) 222

UPS 108

USA *see* United States of America

V

value added tax (VAT) 91, 104, 117, 119

virtual office 135-6

   locations *see* Regus

virtual personal assistant (PA) 138-9

virtual phone number 137-8

W

weak pound, benefits of 5, 6

webinar(s) 35-6, 125

what to pack when travelling 142-3

Y

YouTube 53

Other Books by Emma Jones

Spare Room Start Up

How to start a business from home

Have you ever dreamt of starting your own business? Dreamt of working from home, a ten-second commute, the flexibility to work when you want to, and the joy of being your own boss? This book can show you how to turn those dreams into reality in just a few simple steps.

With serial entrepreneur and home business expert Emma Jones as your guide, you will discover just how easy it is to start and run a successful business from your spare room.

Organised by three key themes – business, lifestyle and technology – *Spare Room Start Up* provides you with simple solutions and demonstrates the ease and low cost with which a home business can be started. Find out how you too can enjoy the rewards of running a home business whilst leading a happier and healthier life.

www.harriman-house.com/spareroomstartup

Available Formats:

Paperback
ISBN:9781905641680

Working 5 to 9

How to start a successful business in your spare time

Emma Jones, founder of the home business website Enterprise Nation and author of *Spare Room Start Up*, delves into the working 5pm to 9pm trend and profiles 60 people who are running successful businesses outside of their normal office hours, everything from writing, baking and accounting, to magic, music and even pig farming! She offers over 50 ideas of businesses you can run in your spare time and looks at franchise ideas that can be run in the same way.

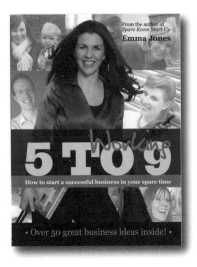

There's advice on starting a business, sales, marketing, technology and how to maintain your social life whilst working 5 to 9.

www.harriman-house.com/working5to9

Available Formats:

Paperback
ISBN:9781906659684

ePub eBook
ISBN:9780857190543

Coming 2011...

The Start-Up Kit

Everything you need to start and run a business

The *Start-Up Kit* contains everything you need to start and run your own business!

At its heart is a book covering all aspects of starting up – from developing a business idea and setting up a company to marketing your new business, getting that first sale and making the most of the latest tech developments. Full of great advice from start-up expert Emma Jones and packed with case studies from people who've already started their own successful businesses.

The kit also contains some amazing offers from some of the leading brands for small business.

www.brightwordpublishing.com

Available from early 2011

Available Formats:

Paperback
ISBN:ISBN:9781908003010